# CRICKET GALLERY

# CRICKET GALLERY

Fifty profiles of famous players
from *The Cricketer*

Edited by David Frith

FOREWORD BY
HRH PRINCE PHILIP,
DUKE OF EDINBURGH,
KG, KT

Photographs by Patrick Eagar

LUTTERWORTH PRESS
Richard Smart Publishing
in association with *The Cricketer*

First published 1976

Published by Lutterworth Press
Luke House, Farnham Road, Guildford, Surrey
and Richard Smart Publishing
in association with *The Cricketer*

Copyright © The Cricketer Limited, 1976

ISBN 0 7188 7000 X

Printed by Jolly & Barber Limited
Rugby, Warwickshire

# CONTENTS
# AND ILLUSTRATIONS

*Illustrations appear on italicised page numbers*

# ALPHABETICAL LIST
# OF CRICKETERS
# FEATURED

# FOREWORD
## by
## HRH Prince Philip, Duke of Edinburgh, KG, KT

Every sport has its heroes. It is impossible not to admire exceptional skill and talent. But cricket seems to produce an exceptional type of hero. Great cricketers are usually great personalities as well. It may be that a first-class cricketer's life is rather longer than in most sports; there is therefore a better chance to become known. It may also be that cricket is just as much a campaign as a game and the violent fluctuations of fortune demand qualities of character as well as sheer talent.

Whatever it is, the Gallery portraits collected in this book make fascinating reading. It might be assumed that there must be some common denominator in the background of the cricketers who figure in this book. If there is, it has nothing to do with race or climate, riches or poverty, education or coaching. The 'greats' have come through every conceivable avenue to reach the top. The only thing they certainly have in common is a real devotion to the game. Most of them may be professionals in practice and others may have a professional approach but if they do not enjoy the game they do not figure in this book.

# INTRODUCTION

However much the world has squirmed and writhed during the 1970s in the face of violence and disaster, neuroses and shortages, however much humanity has failed to hold to its course of progress, avoiding wanton deviation or ambush, of one thing sports-lovers (so many of whom are escapists anyway) may be certain: the decade so far has seen a generous allocation of high-class cricketers. Seldom if ever has the game been so richly international in that all the Test-playing countries have fielded strong teams, in some cases perhaps their strongest ever. These years may have seen the banishment from Test cricket of South Africa, yet even as this book goes into production there are encouraging signs that the three cricket control bodies of that nation may soon unify and thus open the way for multi-racial cricket to be played by and throughout South Africa. Re-entry to international competition is then presumed to be a formality.

The Gallery series began in *The Cricketer* in February 1970, when the magazine, already entering its fiftieth year, was edited by E. W. Swanton. The feature was instantly popular. Other regular features have come and gone during the six years, but Gallery has become an institution.

Cricketers have considered selection as a Gallery subject to be not the least acceptable of accolades, and the 'pin-up' photographs, usually (and in this volume *all*) the work of Patrick Eagar, have been popular vessels for the players' autographs. There have been so many fine

11

first-class cricketers afield during the 1970s that some favourites will inevitably have missed inclusion. There is still time. Topicality is not the sole consideration before selection.

The series began long enough ago for there to be a need of footnotes. The reader may find some quaint twists in these little postscripts, which disclose some of the subsequent fortunes no more apparent to subject and writer at the time of original publication than can be any other particles of the future when a writer puts pen to paper, advisedly expounding the past while studiously avoiding any prognostication.

This collection, then, reflects cricket in the 'seventies through the personalities and the performances of the game's leading exponents. The men and their moments are portrayed – often fondly – by a 'gallery' of writers whose own love of cricket is clearly revealed. Happily, most of the cricketers themselves will bestride the world's cricket grounds for some seasons to come. Others hardly yet heard of will join them and replace them . . . but that can wait until a companion volume a good few years from now.

DAVID FRITH

Guildford, 1976

# COLIN COWDREY

## by Alan Ross

*The Cricketer* February 1970

As I write this, it is 15 years to the day that Colin Cowdrey made his first, and possibly most remarkable, Test century; 102 out of 191 in the third Test, at Melbourne, in 1954. Hutton, Edrich, May and Compton had gone to Miller and Lindwall for 20, and only a batsman of superb technique and complete composure could have survived long on such a wicket against such bowling. Cowdrey was 22, playing in his first Test series. 'His century,' I wrote at the time, 'had the bloom of youth on it; but the soil from which it sprang had been tended lovingly and long . . . [it was] a blend of leisurely driving and secure back play, of power and propriety.' Two runs later Cowdrey was out, playing no stroke and being bowled off his pads. The glory and the indignity, through the years, came somehow to seem typical.

Among the great English batsmen of the post-war period – Hutton, Compton, Washbrook, May, Dexter, Graveney, Barrington – Cowdrey, I suppose, has looked about the best 'bred'. Yet with breeding – the inherited grace and effort-lessness that combine to form the grand manner – and the assumption of authority without tokens of display that is another characteristic, there has gone mildness, indeci-sion, a stubborn passivity. I cannot think of a great player harder to coax into awareness of his reserves, nor one who, in the mood, made the art of batsmanship seem more art-less, more a mere extension of his own geniality. At his best he was a dolphin among minnows, gambolling between the green and the blue as if cares were not invented, almost patronising. At his less good he seemed imprisoned by some interior gaoler, feet chained, arms pinioned, shuffling away a long sentence.

More than most he is a mood player, delicate in his responses to the invisible strings of memory and music. A false note and he is becalmed, devoid of will and wizardry. Lesser players create their own context, impose their wishes on unpropitious elements, defy luck and roughness of touch. John Edrich is one such. Others, like May and Dexter, had a savagery of stroke that, once achieved, meant business. Cowdrey, like Graveney, has preferred to succeed or fail on his own terms, narcissistically declining to disfigure his own reflection, never hurrying, never bringing brute strength to the caressive lullaby of his strokeplay. His refusal to hit himself into form, or in mid-innings to demolish an attack, has often been maddening; sweet words when one wanted to see the big stick, reason when one hungered for violence. He could not, I imagine, be otherwise. Sometimes it has paid off, sometimes not. As captain and batsman he has, through injury, ineffectiveness and inability to turn the screw that last fraction, missed chances galore; yet, in the final analysis, his accomplishments have been immense, his achievements legion, his consistency, chivalry and charm of character unique.

'In the final analysis?' It is, at the start of 1970, a dubious moment to pronounce such phrases. Is this longest of post-war Test careers already over, or is the most glittering prize, victory in Australia under his leadership, still ahead? They say they never come back, but Cowdrey has, more than once, and if I had to bet on it I would, on balance, just take him to do so again.

He has, over the years, changed surprisingly little, being of that outwardly heavy build and solid gait that announces itself and the maturity it represents almost from the outset. In his round, sallow features the jester and the monk share a gravity of vocation; in his behaviour at slip, his walk between overs and his running between wickets, the ferryboat and the racing yacht share aptitudes.

My first overseas tour as cricket correspondent of *The Observer* was also Cowdrey's first as a player, so that, uniquely, he has been a major part of all the Test cricket I have covered. We share, too, a background of India and

Colin Cowdrey

Oxford, not particularly relevant except that it meant I warmed to him early on and remember his hundred for Oxford at Lord's as clearly as if it was yesterday. I cherish it with his 1954 Melbourne hundred, his superb batting in West Indies in 1959-60, and countless other purple passages in his hundred Test matches, to say nothing of his marvellous virtuosity at slip, as among the most enhancing images in my cricket experience.

He has, as few do, elaborated his technique, added new strokes (such as the latest effective but hideous scoop to long leg), refined old ones. His driving between point and mid-off, with minimal movement of the feet and gentle dismissiveness of the bat, is tidal in its rhythmic inevitability, its oceanic break. He can hook, when roused, with affronted grandeur. He cuts with the kind of glee sadistic surgeons bring to complex incisions or a wild conductor to the resuscitation of anaemic arpeggios.

He has brought to the cricket of his time high ideals, impeccable manners an engaging presence. He has blossomed and bumbled, conjured rare tunes out of stodgy skies, suggested the richest of ports, the lightest of soufflés. He would have made my life happier if he had played for Sussex instead of Kent, but, that apart, most of the regrets in his career fade into insignificance compared to the shining rewards. He has in his comfortable way had to accommodate himself to many uncomfortable experiences; but though he has never, in a material fashion, had to struggle, I believe he has a sense of values and enough insight, if pushed deeply into himself and able to come to terms with more astringent concepts, to offset some of the deader wood at the top of the cricket tree.

*Colin Cowdrey, the 'dolphin among minnows', announced his retirement from full-time first-class cricket at the end of the 1975 season. He had gone to Australia for a fifth time, in 1970–71, as MCC vice-captain to Illingworth. Then in the winter of 1974–75 the cricket world was taken aback when he was called for as emergency replacement in the ailing, shellshocked England side. His patience, technique and courage against Lillee and Thomson justified the choice –*

*which, significantly, had been that of the senior players themselves. With a record 114 Test caps, 7624 runs, and 120 catches, Cowdrey's escutcheon is mounted high in a place of honour in Test match annals. In all first-class cricket he recorded over 40,000 runs and a century of centuries.—Ed.*

# GRAEME POLLOCK

## by Michael Melford

*The Cricketer* April 1970

This is the age of competence and solid application rather than of genius and magic, so the presence of Graeme Pollock among the world's great batsmen is all the more striking. Where other successful batsmen eliminate mistakes by not attempting anything outside their proven range, he recognises few limits and backs his extra ability to see him through.

The easily-seen resemblance to another tall left-hander with a full majestic swing of the bat, a certain Frank Woolley, established him at an early age as something out of the ordinary. His remarkable precocity – according to his father he could walk at eight months – the power and range of his strokes and the grandeur of some of his most famous innings have confirmed him as a batsman who would have adorned any age. The bare statistics he will leave behind may not be unbeatable (in six seasons up to the end of 1969 he had played in only 19 Test matches. In the same period Bill Lawry had played in 48), but in full cry Graeme Pollock can make other world-class batsmen look very ordinary mortals.

He was nineteen when he arrived in Australia in 1963, made 100 in Perth in 88 minutes, and played other innings which are reliably reported to have had hard-boiled Australian observers on their feet cheering. The ease with which he took the step to the top was no surprise to those who had seen him already in South Africa and England.

There was mild concern in his family of talented games players in Port Elizabeth when at the age of three he firmly gripped the bat left-handed, for he does everything else right-handed. However, his father, who kept wicket in his time for the Orange Free State, had been similarly

Graeme Pollock

inclined. He was in the school side on his thirteenth birthday and, at 16 years and 335 days, became the youngest batsman to make 100 in the Currie Cup. He was no less precocious in other games. One reason for Graeme's early maturity could be that throughout his boyhood he was bowled at by a future Test fast bowler, his brother Peter.

George Cox of Sussex, coaching at Grey High School, was one of those who had the delicate job of guiding the genius in the right direction, and when Graeme Pollock came to England in 1961 with his family, he played a few matches for Sussex Second XI. At about this time he acquired the final two-and-a-half inches over six feet and, as someone who saw him play that summer said, he was a very surprising seventeen-year-old.

A year later he was making 209 not out at Port Elizabeth against the late Ron Roberts's Cavaliers, and a year after that he was in Australia. Of his two Test 100s there, the second was an extraordinary innings of 175. In four hours 43 minutes he and Barlow scored 341, a record stand for any wicket in South African Test history.

His first encounters with the MCC spinners, Titmus and Allen, in 1964–65 were on turning pitches and the honours were with the bowlers. But he finished the series by making 137 and 77 not out in the last Test, and in England a few months later he played what must be reckoned one of the decisive innings in Test history. At Trent Bridge in the second Test he took on the English in their own conditions and, with his brother, who took ten wickets, beat them.

On the sort of damp overcast day on which English bowlers are wont to confound or subdue the best visiting batsmen, he made 125 out of 160 in two hours 20 minutes. In only 70 minutes after lunch he made 91 out of 102. South Africa, who had been floundering at 43 for 4 against Cartwright, were taken to a score of 269 which won them match and series. In sophisticated bowling circles you hear this innings decried as 'lucky' and 'mere slogging', but it transformed the match in a couple of hours. I would have thought than any great batsman would have been proud to have played it against a bowler of Cartwright's skill operating with everything in his favour.

His batting in the present series against Australia, with his greatest single achievement to date, 274 in 420 minutes at Durban, speaks for itself. Against Australia in the great series of 1966-67, Pollock played two innings which especially demonstrated the full range of his remarkable technique. The first was his 90 in 90 minutes at Johannesburg. I remember him moving nimbly down a fast pitch and hitting two sixes and 15 fours, mostly off the front foot.

At Cape Town a week later he had a pulled thigh muscle, and on a slower pitch made 209 almost entirely off the back foot. His skill in finding the gaps on either side of the wicket off the back foot brought him 100 in only 139 balls, and only then did he attempt anything off the front foot. A feature of this innings was the ease with which he played a shot to the long hop, lying back to lift it high and straight, rather than towards midwicket where most batsmen will hit it.

He can descend from the sublime to the earthy with a bump. The Johannesburg innings ended with a fearful swish at a ball which bowled him behind his legs; he has several characteristics reminiscent of Denis Compton: his running between wickets seldom allows his admirers to relax, and he can communicate to them with peculiar clarity his confidence or concern. He can sometimes be prised out through impatience: against accurate spin he will be looking to drive off the back foot anything which is a fraction short of a length. If it does not come, he may get out through taking a liberty with a ball not quite short enough.

Like Denis Compton, too, Graeme Pollock keeps the bowlers interested as well as the public. When they have been struck for 101 in 52 minutes, as was a reputable Barbados attack at Scarborough last September, or if, like one Australian fast bowler, they have to suffer the indignity of an enormous straight drive on to a roof far behind them, they may be luke-warm in their enthusiasm. But at least they are being given a chance in fair and exhilarating combat.

*The exhilaration of combat – at Test match level – was over for Graeme Pollock, had he but known it. South Africa's isolation, begun in 1968, was completed by the cancellation of the 1970 tour. South Africa was outlawed, and thenceforth Pollock, together with most other top-line Springboks, was to play only domestic cricket, where the challenges were less strident. During the years that followed, he issued frequent reminders of his great gifts, as in a record Gillette Cup innings of 222 not out at Port Elizabeth, where he later took two glorious centuries off the Derrick Robins XI's bowling in one and the same match.—Ed.*

# TOM GRAVENEY
## by J. M. Kilburn

*The Cricketer* May 1970

Tom Graveney has always looked a cricketer of the West Country, though he was born in Northumberland. His schooldays were passed in Bristol, and when they were over he chose voluntary Army service before conscription, to reach commissioned rank. By the time he returned to Bristol in 1947 his elder brother, Ken, had become a Gloucestershire player, and Tom was introduced to the county club as 'a kid brother I can't bowl out'.

Cricket was not a compulsion for Tom Graveney. He had talent that encouraged him towards a career in professional golf, and he had opportunity to train in accountancy. He accepted cricket and satisfied anticipations as a batsman of uncommon grace and authority. By 1951 he was playing for England.

On appearance alone Graveney's place in England teams could never have been questioned. His batting, founded on the classical forward strokes, contained an elegance that distinguished him even in the highest company, and when derivations were sought for his style, Hammond was invariably the quoted model.

In fact Graveney could have drawn inspiration only from Hammond's name. The two players were not contemporary and resemblance in the eye of beholders was beauty seen and beauty remembered.

Graveney's early international career was unspectacular without being unsuccessful, but ironically his successes sowed doubts of his adequacy; he did enough to create assumptions that he should be doing more. By the most exacting standards he was found wanting in critical moments, lacking concentration at the crunch. He was discarded for the vital matches in the 1954–55 tour of Australia, and modest performances in the Test rubbers immediately following brought depreciation, with regret but not injustice.

Whenever Graveney was out of the England side England cricket was not necessarily weakened but it seemed slightly unrepresentative, as a June garden without roses or a banquet without wine. Roses blossomed and wine was relished in innings of 258 and 164 against West Indies in 1957, but another tour of Australia was disappointing and Graveney left the Test match scene for three years.

They were years of disturbance in his county cricket. He left Gloucestershire to join Worcestershire, but immediate registration for his new county was not permitted and he had to endure the summer of 1961 without appearing in the Championship. Success for Worcestershire and against Pakistan earned a third tour of Australia, but the outcome was disappointing and again a cricketer of international quality passed into the international wilderness.

Graveney emerged from his experiences a harder, grimmer player. Worcestershire's Championship contention stiffened his sense of batting responsibility; advancing age in itself eliminated some of the batting frivolities. In 1966 England lost the first Test to West Indies, and they turned back to Graveney as ten years earlier they had turned back to Washbrook and to Compton. The parallels were remarkable. Washbrook scored 98 in his innings of recall, Compton scored 94, and Graveney scored 96. Washbrook and Compton met the needs of a specific hour; Graveney stayed to build a new international reputation.

He played Test innings of substance and dignity and charm at home and in West Indies, and he remained an unquestioned selection until he fell into contractual dispute during the Old Trafford Test of 1969.

Graveney may have disappointed some cricketers by playing in Graveney's way, but he has adorned cricket. In an age preoccupied with accountancy he has given the game warmth and colour and inspiration beyond the tally of the scorebook. He has been of the orchard rather than the forest, blossom susceptible to frost but breathtaking in the sunshine.

Figures give him too little credit and too much. They

Tom Graveney

rate him among the most prolific of scorers with a hundred centuries achieved, and ignore the failures to command where command was expected in a critical hour. They obscure serenity and fragility alike. Figures cannot convey the splendour of an evening's innings or the anti-climax of first-over dismissal next morning.

Graveney's batting has always been open-handed and open-hearted, though not always open-eyed. He has tended to read Test match and festival in the same context, his cricket a medium for uncomplicated contest of talent with his own gifts offering an opportunity but not an obligation to succeed. Graveney has presented his ability without enforcing its acceptance. He has felt no guilt in edging a slip catch, because error is a human frailty and he has never sought to eliminate the humanity from cricket.

The difference between his earlier and later batting, indicated by more marked stability, represents not so much a change of heart or change of method as a restriction of adventurous activity through the insistence of advancing years. Graveney has not attempted to circumscribe himself; the swing of his bat has been reduced by the natural process of age, and he still counts cricket in all its forms a game to be enjoyed. Taking enjoyment as it came he has given enjoyment that will warm winters of memory.

*Tom Graveney played in the last of his 79 Test matches against West Indies in 1969, and took up a post as coach to the Queensland Cricket Association that winter, playing in Sheffield Shield cricket. He and his family returned to England in 1972. His 122 centuries and 47,793 runs are records for post-war cricket.—Ed.*

# ALAN KNOTT

## by John Arlott

*The Cricketer* June 1970

There has never been any doubt about the quality of Alan Knott, who now seems likely to keep wicket for Kent and England for the rest of his active life.

As long ago as 1963, county dressing-room intelligence had it that a young wicketkeeper-batsman in the Kent Second XI was a likely prospect. In the next season, just 18, he was brought into the first team for a couple of matches in June and then given a 'run' in August. Against Lancashire at Blackpool he made five catches in the first innings, two in the second; and he turned the course of Kent's last match of the season – with Somerset, who, after dominating the first two days, had reduced the Kent second innings to 58 for 5 and seemed sure to win. Then, with that blend of ability and temperament which characterises his cricket, Knott – top scorer with 55 – began a revival which carried Kent to 247 and a win by 52 runs.

His predecessor, Tony Catt, emigrated to South Africa soon afterwards, and in 1965 Alan Knott made 74 catches and 10 stumpings; scored 559 runs, including an innings of 49 not out against Sussex, which excited everyone who saw it; was capped by Kent; selected by the Cricket Writers' Club as the Best Young Cricketer of the Year; and was discussed by sound critics as England's next wicketkeeper.

The MCC Under-25 matches in Pakistan, 1966–67, were a proving ground for him: on a dispiriting tour he retained heart and humour, batted with greater purpose and effect than several of the specialist batsmen and kept wicket with skill and joy.

His first Test was the second of 1967 against Pakistan: he made seven catches there, and then five and a stumping in the last match of the rubber at The Oval. He had played himself onto the tour of the West Indies, but not into the

England team for the first three Tests. From past experience, Parks had been a calculated selection as a wicketkeeper-batsman on the hard pitches of the Caribbean, but, apart from his 42 in the first Test, he batted unconvincingly and, after three drawn games, Knott was brought in at Port-of-Spain. He kept wicket well, as everyone expected; but, ironically, his previously discounted batting virtually decided the series. West Indies scored 526, and the English first innings was dangerously poised at 260 for 5 when he came in to Cowdrey and stayed to make 69 not out— highest score but one— in a total of 414 from which, after Sobers's declaration, England won the only finished match of the series. He saved the last Test and the rubber with it when he batted four hours for 73 not out, and England held out for a draw with only one wicket standing.

All five Tests against Australia in 1968; a place on the ill-fated Pakistan tour of 1968–69 – on which he had the unique ill-luck of being 96 not out when the third Test was abandoned because of rioting. Last summer he played in all six Tests of the two series, against West Indies – in which he was John Hampshire's partner in the stand which saved the England batting at Lord's and was given the award for the Man of the Series – and New Zealand. Twenty-four years old this spring, he has now played in 18 Tests, made 52 catches and eight stumpings and scored 666 runs at an average of 30.

Kent have been fortunate in their sequence of wicketkeepers – Huish, Hubble, Ames, Levett and Evans. Alan Knott faces the records of Leslie Ames, who scored more runs than any other wicketkeeper in either Test or first-class cricket, and Godfrey Evans, who was responsible for more dismissals than any other player in Tests. They will not daunt him.

Dark, quick-eyed, lithe, neat and fast-moving, he is as lively as Evans; though less extrovert, he has the same buoyancy and the same capacity for providing a psychological fillip for his team-mates at trying times. He walks like an athlete, laughs easily, and is a personable reflection of all that is best in the young men of the 'sixties and

Alan Knott

'seventies. He has proved his ability to stand firm at a crisis; his opponents know, too, that he can be courteously generous about their achievements.

He is a wicketkeeper first, an all-round wicketkeeper without distinguishable weakness. His work is economical, he is well balanced, quick to start, and acrobatic in his ability to dive or jump for distant catches. He works close to the stumps to slow bowling, and takes his friend, contemporary and county colleague Derek Underwood with fine understanding; but he also emerges well from the most searching test of a wicketkeeper, which is off-break bowling to a right-hand batsman.

His batting is alert and confident, marked by quick reactions and lively footwork and, though it is informed by an enterprising approach, it is sufficiently correct in its fundamentals, against both speed and spin, for him to play major defensive innings at Test level.

He scored over a thousand runs in the season of 1968, but there was something of a falling away in his batting last season so that at times he seemed too highly placed in the batting order at number three for Kent and six for England. The gifts of a natural batsman, however, are clearly to be seen in him, and he was entitled to the reaction season that even the best players have experienced. Meanwhile he will, no doubt, persevere, in the nets, with his off-spin bowling; we may suspect that he has been told of Alfred Lyttelton, who discarded his pads in a Test and took four Australian wickets for 19 runs.

*Five years later Alan Knott had taken his figures to 199 catches and 16 stumpings in 73 Test matches, and still remained, at the age of 29, unchallenged as England's wicketkeeper. Frequently his batting saw his side through crises or turned strong positions into virtual victories. During the stormy 1974–75 series he became the only wicketkeeper apart from Kent forerunner Les Ames to score a century in England–Australia Tests.—Ed.*

# GARFIELD SOBERS

## by John Arlott

*The Cricketer* July 1970

For a few months of 1969, out of sheer weariness, Garfield Sobers ceased to produce the figures of the finest cricketer of modern times. Like all such lapses, his failure prompted little men to berate the great. His lack of success is unquestionable, but it no more detracts from the historic fact of his eminence than some indifferent verses make Coleridge less than a great poet. The only remarkable fact about Sobers's bad spell was that it did not occur sooner under the heaviest sustained strain any cricketer has ever known.

No-one who has watched him for any appreciable period can doubt that he is the finest all-rounder in the world. Merely to see him come out on the field, his long, hungry stride a strangely tigerish blend of the relaxed and the purposeful, is to recognise a great athlete. Most would agree, too, that he is the most giftedly versatile player the game has ever known. At Test level he has scored more runs than all but five men, all batsmen, pure and simple, in the entire history of the game; only eight bowlers have taken more wickets and three players have made more catches. No-one approaches his triple record.

Figures, however, tell only part of the story: they cannot show that he is an excitingly brilliant player yet, also, essentially effective. In six different ways – as batsman, fast-medium bowler, finger-spinner, wrist-spinner, close fieldsman and captain – he has taken up cricket matches and remoulded them to his own design. No aspect of his cricket has been more amazing than his capacity for combining quality and quantity of effort; it is as if a single creature had both the class of a Derby-winner and the stamina of a mule. He is the only man ever to have performed the 'impossible' double of 1000 runs and

31

50 wickets in an Australian season – and he did it twice.

There can never have been such an all-round perfor-mance as his in the 1966 West Indies-England series. In the first Test he scored 161, bowled 49 overs for three wickets and West Indies won: at Lord's, where he and Holford, by their long, unfinished sixth-wicket stand made a draw against all probability, he had innings of 46 and 163 not out and one wicket in 43 overs: at Trent Bridge, the second West Indian win, 3 and 94, five wickets in 80 overs: at Leeds, in the match which decided the rubber, he made 174 and bowled 39 overs for eight wickets. When, at The Oval, it seemed as if the side suddenly relaxed after win-ning the series, he scored 81 and 0 and, in England's only innings, took three wickets. His overall figures for the series: 722 runs, average 103, 20 wickets at 27.25 off 269.4 overs. He made ten catches, and captained the side skil-fully and perceptively.

So it was not surprising that, when England went to the West Indies in 1967-68, he decided, after the first three Tests had been drawn, to back himself to bring off another win by his own efforts. At Port-of-Spain he made the decla-ration which brought down on him the condemnation of all those who bemoan lack of enterprise in the modern crick-eter. Everyone remembers that England won the match by seven wickets and took the rubber with it. Not so many recall the efforts of Sobers to draw the series in the final match. He scored 152 and 95 not out, bowled 68 overs for six wickets and pressed England so hard that they held on for a draw with only one wicket standing. He came straight from those matches to England to take up the captaincy of Nottinghamshire. They had been fifteenth in the Cham-pionship table of 1967; in Sobers's first season they were fourth – their highest for 36 years: Sobers was first in the batting averages, second in the bowling, took more catches than anyone else except the wicketkeeper – and hit six sixes from a six-ball over.

He had never played a full English county season before – and instant registration has demonstrated how tiring even experienced players can find it at first encounter. Sobers needed a rest: instead, he took an ageing West

Garfield Sobers

Indian team to Australia. He did his utmost to shore it up; with six wickets in the last innings he played a major part in the side's only Test win; he scored more runs than anyone else, took more wickets than all but Gibbs, but his team simply was not good enough. In the series with New Zealand, for the first time since he entered Test cricket at the age of seventeen, Garfield Sobers knew no success. He never played a major innings and only at the end did he muster a bowling spell of his usual sharpness: for the first time West Indies failed to win a rubber against New Zealand.

He was still nervously weary, and sometimes less than fit, when he came on to England for West Indies' short tour last summer. At Lord's and Leeds he bowled like his former splendid self but, in that losing series, he showed neither the concentration not the confidence of the batsman who holds the record for the highest individual score in Test cricket. Back at Trent Bridge, however, he seemed to find his feet again and the winter's rest must have soothed and renewed him. It would be appropriate if the most highly paid, and first truly international, cricketer should come back – rested, refreshed and married – to re-establish himself at the start of the new decade.

*Garfield Sobers was knighted for services to cricket in the New Year's Honours, 1975, having retired from full-time cricket. His Test record stands alone: 93 matches, 8032 runs at 57.78, highest score 365 not out, 26 centuries, 235 wickets at 34.03, 110 catches. He played successfully in the Central Lancashire League in 1975, and that autumn announced he would play no more competitive cricket. Among his many honours was the Lawrence Trophy for the fastest century of the season – for Notts against Derbyshire in 1974.—Ed.*

# BRIAN CLOSE

## by J. M. Kilburn

*The Cricketer* August 1970

Bitter-sweet has been the characteristic flavour of Brian Close's cricket career. He has stretched his fingertips to clouds of glory and stumbled in a morass of disappointment and controversy. He has enjoyed the highest distinctions and suffered salt in deep wounds. In twenty years he has known few seasons of quiet content.

He was born at Rawdon near Leeds into a cricketing family and his youthful sporting talent was so pronounced that he was plunged into county and Test cricket at the age of 18. Hindsight indicates that too much was undoubtedly asked of him too soon, but true kindness would have involved some cruelty had he been denied the opportunity to score 1000 runs and take 100 wickets and to play for England against New Zealand in his first season of 1949.

Controversy was thrust on him in 1950 when he was selected to tour Australia during his period of National Service. His mere presence in the side attracted public comment and his performances concentrated it.

He scored 108 not out in the opening first-class match and 0 and 1, in culpable fashion, in his only Test. Long before the end of the tour Close had become a cricketing reject.

His climb to rehabilitation was long and slow and was not advanced by personal decisions that discounted well-meant advice and proved unfortunate in outcome. He hoped for a profitable career in professional football and lost a season's cricket through football injury. He drifted into a state of inconsequential performance verging on the fatalistic. In success he was impressive; in failure he appeared to cultivate indifference.

Occasional undertakings for England failed to stifle misgivings, and a dramatic batting error against Australia at Old Trafford in 1961 seemed to confirm a widespread belief that temperament would always wither the blossom of his talent.

Inherent talent was not questioned. Set against all the left-hand batsmen of his time Close looked comparable with the best in artistry, in power and in potential.

Confining himself within the range of the orthodox he was majestic, but he allowed an impression to grow of accomplishment unharnessed and of immaturity extending far beyond cricketing adolescence. His play suggested that he had not found its purpose.

Yorkshire appointed Close their captain in 1963 because the office was vacant and because professional seniority gave him claim to succession. Within one season he had proved himself brilliantly successful. Clearly exercising authority, shrewd in tactics and leading by example at the crease and in the field, Close not only inspired Yorkshire but invigorated himself. In the five Test matches against West Indies he was a resolute batsman, an innings of 70 at Lord's touching the heroic. At the end of the season Close was a tired cricketer, mentally and physically, but he knew the satisfactions of fulfilment.

He was not required in another Test series until 1966 and then only for the last match of a rubber already decided. West Indies had won three of the first four matches and depression had settled over England cricket when Close was given the leadership of a reconstituted side.

His experience was characteristically dramatic. England won the match and Close's captaincy was rated a decisive factor in the result. A new world of promise was opening to him in his 36th year.

It was shattered in 1967. As captain of Yorkshire, Close wanted the County Championship and as captain of England he wanted Test match success over India and Pakistan, not only for its own sake but in preparation for a tour of West Indies and for the visit of Australia in 1968.

By mid-August Yorkshire were Championship leaders but only by such a narrow margin that two points from a drawn game at Edgbaston were balanced against opprobrium for delaying tactics in the field when Warwickshire

Brian Close

were trying to force victory. Yorkshire's conduct was publicly condemned and on the eve of the last Test against Pakistan Close was held responsible in a formal rebuke.

He was not invited to captain MCC in West Indies and in 1968 he did not lead England against Australia. He had lost foothold, again, on the slippery pathway of esteem.

Through all the vicissitudes of his career he has never lost the appreciation of cricketers for talented performance, for investigation of the game's possibilities and for unflinching physical courage.

Close as a young player raised a thrill of delight in response to his powerful and confident left-hand batting, his easy right-arm action for off-spin or swing bowling and his agility in the field. He was handsome in all his athletic pursuits.

Close in mid-career drifted away to the fringes of distinction because his batting too rarely reflected the full extent of his ability and his bowling talent was not consolidated into artistry under discipline. By the evidence of his best innings no England side should have been complete without him, yet his intermittent appearances could not be counted an injustice.

Appointment to captaincy turned self-assurance into channelled purpose. Close was never a more impressive cricketer, in technique and temperament, than when he assumed the responsibilities of leading Yorkshire.

*Brian Close joined Somerset in 1971 and became the county's captain in 1972, a season which saw his appointment as captain of England in the one-day internationals against Australia. His strong leadership was acknowledged then and again when he took charge of Derrick Robins' XI in South Africa. His dedication and iron control were too much for some at Somerset, a county of young players, in 1975, but he was reappointed to lead in 1976, when he will be 45 years old.—Ed.*

# RAY ILLINGWORTH

## by Trevor Bailey

*The Cricketer* September 1970

They say that it's a funny old game and there can be few better examples of the strange quirks that cricket can play than the remarkable transformation in the career of Ray Illingworth in the last two seasons. It really all started a couple of winters ago, when Tony Lock decided not to return to England the following summer and Leicestershire suddenly found themselves without their captain and leading spin bowler. About the same time Ray Illingworth told Yorkshire that he was not satisfied with their terms and asked to be released. They reluctantly agreed to his request and thus provided the Midland county with an ideal substitute.

The general view was that Leicester had made a very shrewd appointment. Ray was probably the most reliable English all-rounder in county cricket with a fine knowledge of the game and tactically very sound. It seemed probable that his international career was over, which certainly did not worry his new employers who wanted him to take them to the top of the Championship. After all he had represented England on 30 occasions without ever quite establishing himself an automatic choice. He had been rather unfortunate that three of his contemporaries, Titmus, Allen, and Mortimore, were off-spinners, who had all gained the reputation of being more effective bowlers abroad. Leicester felt that Ray's bowling would gain them a number of points, as on a helpful pitch he is a match-winner, his batting would provide the solidity to a middle order which had a tendency to fold, and as a captain of the Foreign Legion he would (like Tony Lock) be able to rekindle the enthusiasm and confidence in themselves.

What nobody, including Ray himself, realised was the far-reaching effects this move was to have on English cricket and that, in his very first season with his new club, he would be chosen to lead England, and in the following one be awarded the supreme honour of taking the side to Australia.

Since Ray became captain of England, as a result of Colin Cowdrey's injury, many people have expressed considerable surprise at the effectiveness and authority of his batting, because they regarded him as a highly efficient, and, in certain circumstances, deadly bowler and merely a competent middle-order county batsman. This does not do his prowess with the willow justice, as I have discovered for myself on a number of occasions. Ray did in fact score his first century against Essex and has shown a marked partiality for our bowling ever since. I have lost count of the times, after my county had achieved a breakthrough with the new ball, that we have been unable to press home our advantage because of his arrival at the crease. He has always been exceptionally good against seam bowling and clearly relished leading a recovery. This is perhaps not surprising when one realises that Ray began his adult cricket as an opening bat for Farsley and originally went to Yorkshire as a batsman-cum-medium-pace swing bowler.

The reason why Illingworth's batting ability has been underrated is that he has normally gone in at number six or seven for Yorkshire. As they were one of the strongest teams in the Championship while he was with them, this has automatically reduced his opportunities of playing a big innings on a good pitch, because the earlier batsmen had normally climbed aboard the run waggon before he arrived at the wicket. It is significant that he scored most runs when he was allowed to bat at number five, but with the northern county's batting line-up this was seldom possible and, remembering the amount of bowling he had to undertake, was possibly undesirable. Be that as it may, this was partially responsible for reducing his effectiveness, as runs always beget more runs.

At one time Ray, like so many Yorkshiremen, was unhappy against a good leg-spinner, particularly on fast pitches because he preferred to play from the confines of his crease (while Jim Laker trapped him lbw on the back foot on a number of occasions). Now he has blossomed into

Ray Illingworth

a fine player of all types of bowling with an excellent temperament, a sound defence, and an especially fine square cut.

Although Ray began with Yorkshire as a swing bowler, it was not long before he abandoned this for the far more lucrative trade of an off-spinner.

His apprenticeship as a seamer gave him – just as earlier it had done for Jim Laker – a powerful body action which helped him make the odd ball leave the bat – a valuable asset. Like all Yorkshire bowlers his outlook is essentially mean, begrudging every run. His length and line are excellent, while his trajectory, except when he deliberately tosses one up, is low. This means that a batsman has to take positive action against him, if he wishes to score runs, because he will have to wait a very long time for a loose delivery. A favourite Illingworth ploy against a new player is to bring his fieldsmen in to save the single and have no deep midwicket or square leg. He thus challenges the batsman to attempt a lofted stroke and is prepared to concede a boundary if the shot is successful. He is, of course, a complete craftsman in his chosen profession, equally at home over and round the wicket. On a 'turner' he can be devastating, while on good pitches his ability to release the ball close to the stumps from over the wicket is a distinct advantage.

Ray has a thoroughly professional, Yorkshire approach to cricket and his captaincy is rather like his bridge, conventional, sound, and essentially practical. He would never attempt a finesse for a possible over 'trick', if he knew by so doing it could cost him the game. Similarly his calls are based on assessed points, not tram tickets. His captaincy of the England team this summer and last has been admirable, while his personal contribution, as a player, has been both inspiring and considerable. He is not a flamboyant skipper and in fact is inclined towards caution, but he makes few mistakes and, as with his bridge, misses very few 'tricks'.

When Ray established himself in the Yorkshire team, he became a member of an attack which was distinctly volatile, individualistic and liable to explode at any time.

42

Their bowlers reminded me of the Greek guerillas in the war who were united against the Nazis, the common foe, but never harmonised among themselves. Since those days, Ray has matured and has acquired a more philosophical outlook, possibly aided by his position as unofficial shop steward of the Yorkshire side. Above all he has learned toleration, while still retaining the hardness which one would expect, and wish, from an England captain. He ought to, and I think he will, do a good job in Australia, where his quiet, dry, and slightly sardonic humour should prove very helpful.

*Ray Illingworth's triumph as England's leader in Australia in 1970–71 marked the climax of an interesting career. The two-nil victory which won the Ashes was achieved at the cost of some goodwill, but the sequel – the 1972 home series against a stronger Australia – was without blemish, a spectator's series, when Illingworth perhaps did even better to retain the Ashes by a two-all result with an ageing side against opposition appreciably more dynamic than a year earlier. After staying home in the 1972–73 winter, when Tony Lewis took over the England captaincy, Illingworth was put in charge again in 1973; but after England's torrid time against West Indies – when his own form left much to be desired – he was dropped and Mike Denness was chosen to lead England in the Caribbean. Meanwhile, displaying a shrewdness generally acknowledged as unmatched anywhere in the country, Illingworth took Leicestershire to three Benson & Hedges Cup finals, winning in 1972 and 1975, and to victory in the John Player League in 1974. The ultimate triumph came in 1975 when Leicestershire won their first-ever County Championship. Illingworth was made CBE in 1973.—Ed.*

# JOHN SNOW

## by Alan Ross

*The Cricketer* February 1971

In the hierarchy of English Test opening bowlers John Snow, before the present series in Australia, stood just above Bill Voce. In 25 Tests Snow had 99 wickets at an average of 27.51 as against Voce's 98 wickets from 27 Tests at an average of 27.88. You cannot get much closer than that. Near enough, it is four wickets a Test, rather better than Statham, virtually the same as Larwood and Tate, and not quite so good as Trueman, Tyson and Bedser. It is difficult to know whether Snow is not flattered by such a relationship to the great fast bowlers of the post-Great War era, just as it is difficult to know whether there is more in him than meets the eye, or less.

Sometimes, on a routine day at Hove, nothing in him meets the eye at all, for more than any cricketer of comparable talent that I have seen he seems able to switch off completely. Others can look distracted or detached – Dexter, for one – but Snow, in some curious manner that seems almost a Zen or Yoga technique, manages to become non-apparent. When called upon, a pale ghostly presence goes through the motions and retires into his own cloud of unknowing. It is not simply that on these occasions there is nothing to be desired from effort. Every bowler knows that there are times for putting everything in and times for merely bowling a length and line. Snow's time-clock is one of his own adjustment and disconcertingly it bears no relation to the needs of his captain. Most successful bowlers, regardless of the circumstances, give the impression of liking bowling, of hating being taken off. Snow, on the other hand, seems, too often for comfort, to agree to bowl grudgingly, as if some liberty were being taken with his contract. This is, inevitably, more

John Snow

pronounced in county cricket than in Test cricket, and it has made him on the whole a less consistent and willing performer for Sussex than for England.

Yet for all the apparent moodiness of character, the impassivity and aloofness, there he is already in the top half-dozen Test wicket-takers among English fast bowlers. Given a reasonable length of career one would expect him to end up somewhere near Alec Bedser's 236 wickets, not a bad place for anyone. Already, as I write, he has a useful haul of wickets from the first two Tests in Australia, where he has to carry the fast attack almost single-handed as Bedser had to in his day.

In this sense, John Snow is unlucky, for nearly all the great fast bowlers have worked in pairs. Trueman and Statham last played in a Test match in 1965, which was the summer Snow played his first two Tests, one each against South Africa and New Zealand, so that they just overlapped. Since then he has had a series of partners, Brown, Jones, Ward, Higgs, Lever, Shuttleworth, none of them – for one reason or another – quite staying the course or having the necessary hostility.

Snow's Test career took its time to blossom, short spells when he looked a bowler of quality and pace alternating with periods when he looked moderateness itself. Yet he nearly always picked up an early wicket and he could usually make short work of the tail. There was no-one clearly better than him after the departure of Trueman and Statham, though Brown was the more persevering, and Jones, Larter and Higgs were all preferred to him on the last tour of Australia. It was, as a matter of fact, a dismal period for fast bowlers in England, with scarcely a bowler of genuine pace or swing around, and few with an even tolerable action.

Then, in the West Indies in 1967–68, Snow suddenly took on a new dimension. All over the place in the opening games, so that he was left out of the first Test, he sprang into action on a cracked Sabina Park pitch to take 7 for 49 in the second Test. From this time on he was the fastest, most hostile bowler on either side, dangerous with the bouncer, but equally controlled in length and direction.

46

Next, in Barbados, he took 5 for 86 and 3 for 39 in a drawn match. In the fifth Test his figures of 4 for 82 and 6 for 60 gave him a final haul of 27 wickets from four Tests, as good as any bowler has managed in the West Indies.

From this moment on, Snow has been England's first choice as a fast bowler, though he has not always looked it around the county grounds of England. Probably he needs the stimulus of a Test match to find the resources that separate him from a dozen bowlers not far short of his average form. (Or the stimulus of being 'rested' from a Test match, as he was in 1969 against New Zealand, when Hampshire got the rough end of his displeasure to the tune of 5 for 29 and 5 for 51.)

The great virtues of Snow as a bowler are his easy, relaxed run-up, his change of pace, his late movement and nip off the pitch – either way, but especially leaving the left-hander – and the steep lift he gets from little short of a length. He shows more of the right shoulder to the batsman than most of the best fast bowlers did, and he has none of the classic expansion – left arm high and right hand coming from far down – of such as Trueman, McKenzie and Tyson, for example. Instead, after an initial scraping of the feet, like a dog at the door, he lopes into a gently accelerating rhythm that achieves tension and menace without evident stress. He is not a genuine swinger of the ball through the air, in the manner of someone like Bailey or Davidson, but his natural movement into the right-hander is often abruptly halted on pitching by movement the other way. When the mood is on him he makes fast bowling seem as natural an activity as breathing, perhaps because he husbands his energies as carefully as Lindwall did and is really quick for no more than a couple of balls an over.

For all his disengaged air at third man Snow is a beautiful mover in the deep, quick to pounce one-handed and fast and accurate in the throw. As a batsman he has had his moments in Test matches, both as defendant and aggressor, especially since he has been obliged to discontinue his imitation of Cowdrey, left pad thrust like a dumpling one way, head turned the other.

It could be seen that John Snow will return from this series in Australia among our most successful bowlers ever to have gone there. He is already on the way to it. Quite what people make of him is another matter, for he is neither a character nor exactly characterless. No-one has found him easy to captain – though I imagine Cowdrey managed it with fewer misgivings than anyone else – so much so that perhaps the real solution would be for him to captain a side himself. It would be worth watching.

*John Snow went on to play an appreciable part in England's 1970–71 victory in Australia, demolishing the home team with 7 for 40 in the fourth Test, at Sydney, where England won by 299 runs, and finishing the series with 31 wickets in six Tests. Difficulties lay ahead. He was disciplined for knocking India's Gavaskar off his feet between wickets in the 1971 Lord's Test, and did nothing to increase his popularity by declaring himself unavailable for the 1972–73 tour of India and Pakistan. He was England's leading wicket-taker (24) against Australia in 1972, but a year later he was discarded. His figures might not have done him justice against West Indies at The Oval, but neither, it seems, did his attitude. For four Test series he remained the people's choice, but not the selectors'. Then in 1975 came recall: for the Prudential World Cup and the Tests against Australia. A good deal of the old fire was there. He was still more than a would-be poet who enjoyed the occasional few overs of fast bowling.—Ed.*

# M. J. K. SMITH

## by Mike Stevenson

*The Cricketer* March 1971

David Brown, the Warwickshire and England fast bowler, writes of Mike Smith: 'I think a young cricketer (and indeed any young man) could not find a better example to follow on and off the field'.

Bill Packer, his cricket and rugby coach at Stamford School, writes of his earliest cricketing days: 'As a captain at school he was superb . . . and boys of his era here have always said that they never enjoyed their cricket so much as they did under Mike's leadership.'

Alan Smith, the Test selector and his present county captain, writes: 'Of course, as a person, he is quite delightful and I don't think you will find anyone in the game who doesn't like him. He is rarely ruffled, always cheerful, easy-going and loyal. He frequently gives the impression of being vague and forgetful and this in itself is a major source of dressing-room laughter.'

Canon Kelly, the principal of his college at Oxford, used to refer to Mike Smith as being 'a model of a modern Admirable Crichton.' Despite the Gilbertian ring of this last panegyrical utterance, it is fairly typical of the universal affection and respect with which this quiet, kindly, amusing and immensely distinguished sportsman is regarded.

Born in Leicestershire at Broughton Astley in 1933, Michael John Knight Smith played for Stamford School before he was 13, scoring 49 against Oakham when his main technical problem was seeing over the top of his pads. His nickname was 'Blondie' and his subsequent successes assume in retrospect something of the flavour of a strip-cartoon.

He played for the XI for six seasons and was its captain for three; at the end of an excellent school career and armed with two grade As, and a grade B at 'A' Level, he attempted to gain entrance to Cambridge University. To their eventual chagrin, I imagine, St John's turned him down – perhaps word had filtered through to Fenner's that he was weak on the off side!

But St Edmund's Hall, Oxford, were glad to have him and he embarked upon a career at his school coach's former college, which ended with his acquiring a good second and a double Blue. Bill Packer writes of a game between St John's and Stamford shortly after Mike's unsuccessful attempt to gain admission: 'When the school played their June fixture later on the St John's ground, Mike really thrashed the bowling, declared, captured four wickets before tea and, largely thanks to his own brilliant close catching, fulfilled his promise to the team that they would be boating by six!'

A trial-match century was followed by another in his first match for the university (against Gloucestershire) and his first-class career, which had begun with three matches for Leicestershire in 1951, was well and truly launched.

His rugby prospered too and he played fly-half for Oxford in 1954 and '55, the latter year seeing the development of his partnership with Onllwyn Brace which caused the elevation of so many interested journalistic eyebrows. Brace's admiring voice can be added to the general chorus: 'In rugby terms he was as blind as a bat! But he was an instinctive player – he must have had built-in radar!' Brace, who described Mike Smith to me as 'the perfect gentleman', paid him the ultimate compliment when he admitted that he was 'sad that he wasn't a Welshman' and as a general view of his rugby-playing ability and potential, claimed that 'if he'd devoted himself entirely to rugby he'd have gone every bit as far as he did in cricket.'

But he went sufficiently far to be selected for England against Wales in 1956, with Brace at scrum-half for Wales. In his first and only international Mike met the Welsh pack in brilliant mood, so that his own forwards spent the afternoon moving backwards. He did not have the happiest of games but uncomfortable memories of this match may be modified by justifiable pride in being the only living

M. J. K. Smith

Englishman to represent his country at both rugby and cricket.

David Brown's view of his captaincy is significant: 'Mike, for my money, is easily the best skipper I have played with. Without driving, he draws more reserves out of a player than any other captain I've known.'

He has been consistently unobtrusive and his dealings with the Press, though presenting his players in a favourable light, have never contributed to his own glorification.

No-one is better qualified to judge him as a purely county captain than Leslie Deakins, the Warwickshire secretary. He wrote in 1967, on the occasion of Mike's 'first' retirement from first-class cricket, of the debt owed him by his county. 'He will not be readily replaced nor easily forgotten and it is certain that the very happy, sometimes successful, sometimes disappointing but never dull 11 years of his captaincy will long be remembered at Edgbaston.'

It was typical of the man that he should spend a considerable amount of time during his short 'retirement' in successfully organising the first National Club Knockout.

As a batsman, he is not quite up to the May, Cowdrey or Hutton standard, but few players' records can compare with his for consistency over the years as any reader of *Wisden* can discover. It was his misfortune as an England player to be miscast, at one stage, as an opening batsman. Wilfred Wooller, a Test selector, writes: 'My own feeling is that Mike should not have been an opener, as he did not pick up the fast delivery quickly enough when he first went in.'

Mike Smith has been adamant about the fact that wearing spectacles has in no way hindered his cricket career; it is interesting to consider this differing view which suggests that his 'built-in radar', which aided him on the rugby field, could not operate with complete success when faced with the initial onslaught of a Hall or a Pollock.

The criticisms that he has from time to time received, of being exclusively an on-side player, seem to me to be largely unfounded; the prevalence of off-spin and inslant bowling caused him to develop on-side play in order to deal with the circumstances that faced him and those who know his batting best are scornful of such a view.

The last innings I watched him play during the past season that saw his welcome return to the first-class game perfectly exemplified his talent; without taking undue risk, he took a single off practically every ball, ran like a frisky colt and scored, from the outset of his innings, at around a run a minute, while his colleague at the other end attempted to hit the cover off the ball and progressed rather more slowly.

To many people, his batting in 1970 was a revelation. What a superb thing it would be if Alan Smith were right and his distinguished namesake were 'about to "do a Graveney"': to be a better batsman in his late 30s than at any time before.'

*Comparatively unheralded, Mike Smith's retirement was announced at the end of the 1975 season. In the hallowed England tradition, he had been recalled to the Test side in 1972, getting a start in all six of his innings and taking two magnificent catches at long leg. Continuing as a valued member of the Warwickshire side, he had scored almost 40,000 runs, with 69 centuries, by the time he put aside his bat at the age of 42.—Ed.*

# CLIVE LLOYD

## by Mike Stevenson

*The Cricketer* May 1971

Whoever it was that described Clive Lloyd as 'a great, gangling, begoggled supercat' must (temporarily at least) have been inspired; nevertheless, he has been in county cricket just long enough to invite our taking him for granted.

Equally readily can be forgotten the immense impact of overseas cricketers from 1968 onwards, after the strict laws governing their inclusion were relaxed. A seasoned professional of the school of 'ritual cricket', writing home thereafter, might have couched his epistle in the following terms:

Old Trafford,<br>Friday, 13th

Dear Mum,

Tell Dad it's a b . . . . . .

We're playing Lancashire first go off and I'm wheeling away on a nice length when this great, bloody bespectacled bully starts belting me over the top as if we was in club cricket. I bowls it a bit shorter and 'e 'ooks me. Then to cap it all, he digs me best yorker out and that goes for 4 an' all.

When we bat, I push to cover to get off the mark and blow me if the flaming idiot doesn't throw down the bowler's wicket before I've got half way.

Eeh! I do wish I'd gone into the shop, like you said.

Love, Joe.

To his admirers, Lloyd must appear unique; yet he belongs to the West Indian tradition as clearly as Sobers, whose influence is clearly written on the younger man (as Sobers, when bowling, transfers the ball from right to left hand before delivery, acknowledging an early debt to Sir Frank Worrell). Surely much of the West Indies' success results from this tendency for the heroes of one generation to be copied by their aspiring juniors.

Clive Lloyd

By contrast, English batting is so cerebrally over-theoretical. 'Open up,' says the coach, 'and take the inswinger on the thigh-pad or let it pass down the leg side.'

'Rubbish!' says a Sobers or a Lloyd. 'I believe in the old-fashioned leg-hit. I may get a top edge every now and again but please note what has happened to a number of reputable bowlers in the meantime.' Clive Lloyd believes (sing Hallelujah!) that attack is almost always the best form of defence.

Should the batsman, subscribing to the Pauline theory that 'all things be done decently and in order', play each ball on its merits? Surely the length ball played with decorum breeds confidence and efficiency in the bowler, whereas the length ball hit on the rise leaves him wondering just where to bowl the next one.

Any bowler confronted with Clive Loyd must know the terrifying fascination of Russian roulette. 'Will it be this one . . . or this one . . . or . . . that one nearly killed me and it's broken the sightscreen!'

One former England player described Lloyd as a 'mere slogger'. Apart from taking exception to the 'mere' (sad that there are so few 'sloggers' among our nines, tens and elevens these days), it is palpably absurd to describe anyone possessing the variety and precision of strokeplay at Lloyd's disposal in such disparaging terms.

A more valid criticism is that (like virtually all players) he is not relatively as good a batsman when the ball is moving as on a plumb 'un. When facing Tom Cartwright on a seamer's wicket at Southport, his batting suggested desperation, if not death-wish; but, to his credit, he got runs.

Certainly he is less vulnerable to the bouncer than he once was and one only has to consider the methods employed by several of the present Australian batsmen, when facing the England attack, to realise that there is a vast difference between periodic uncertainty and impotent capitulation.

Whatever attack he fears, Clive Lloyd tends to get runs or get out; last season he found himself confronted by a couple of medium-pacers clearly intent upon demonstrating his much-publicised Achilles heel. The first time a ball was bounced at him, its next bounce occurred around 40 yards over the long-leg boundary. You can't kill tigers with a toothpick.

However exciting Lloyd's batting, it is his fielding that has already earned him a place among the immortals. With the strings of the puppet slack, he slouches like a double-jointed gangster. (It amazes me that so fine a mover can sometimes look so unathletic.) But seconds, it seems, before an average cover would have moved, the elastic, hunter's stride carries his huge frame to impossibly distant regions, where the telescopic arm will click out and the slick pick-up and shy nudge the poor David of a batsman into belief that Goliath has beaten him to the draw.

Perhaps Lloyd's salient cricketing quality is his unpredictability, something which appears to have spread from his cover-driving to his car-driving, which shares many of the more uninhibited characteristics of the Keystone Cops.

He has enjoyed his time in Lancashire and Lancashire has enjoyed him. His two years at Haslingden in the League made him many friends, among whom is John Ingham: 'We were batting together against Enfield on a freezing day just after Clive had landed. There was a gale too and we'd both been pushing up the line automatically. I thought Clive was in a stupor, when there was an explosion the other end. I'd just time to turn my back before the ball took me on the backside and felled me like an ox.'

A friend of mine said of him: 'I've never known anyone laugh longer or more helplessly': a different view of the man who has so often played the Demon King to Harry Pilling's inimitable Fairy Queen.

But the last word on Clive Lloyd, 26 years old, of Guyana, Lancashire and West Indies, demolition expert, Chan Canasta of covers, consistently under-rated bowler and shy but friendly individual, should be allowed to his county captain. Jack Bond said of him: 'We don't tolerate "stars" in the Lancashire team. Clive has fitted in excellently and he's a great team man.'

Lancashire must be delighted to have acquired a star of Clive Lloyd's brilliance; they must be equally relieved that he resolutely refuses to behave like one.

*Clive Lloyd's proudest moment came on June 21, 1975, when he held aloft the Prudential World Cup, won by his West Indies team after a thrilling final against Australia at Lord's. He made a thunderous 102 in that match; he was already a legend in Gillette Cup cricket, having struck 66 in the 1971 final and a memorable 126 in 1972, and going on to make 73 not out to take the cup to Lancashire yet again in 1975. The sternest challenge came in 1974, when he was chosen to succeed Kanhai as captain of West Indies. He led them through India and Pakistan successfully, hitting a career-best of 242 not out in the decisive fifth Test at Bombay, having signalled his first match as captain with 163 at Bangalore. A year later came the traumatic experience of leading West Indies through Australia, winning only one Test and losing five. He retained the captaincy for the home series against India, doubtless hoping the worst was behind him.—Ed.*

# BARRY RICHARDS

## by Michael Melford

*The Cricketer* June 1971

If you saw Barry Richards in England with the South African schoolboys side in 1963 or three years later with Wilfred Isaacs' XI, you did not have to be very bright to realise that a player of unusual talent was in the process of development. What would have been impossible then was to guess how this genius would flower, for Richards comes of a generation of South African cricketers who are acceptable alone but are treated as fiends incarnate if they travel as a team. Thus he has become a cosmopolitan who sees his future more in Australia and England than at home.

In England, where they view the commercially-minded and the genius with suspicion, he is sometimes looked at warily. It is only now, in his fourth highly successful season with Hampshire, that he is becoming recognised as something out of the ordinary. Like most other great players in England he will not be really lauded as such until he has retired. People in Hampshire are presumably too busy subscribing to the sheep-like platitudes that there is nothing worth watching nowadays to realise that in Richards and Roy Marshall they have had two of the most gifted and attractive players in the world together on their doorstep.

One fascination of Richards' batting lies in its variety of shades. His method when he is applying himself to the full is near perfection. Everything is in the right place, where the textbook directs. But for much of his career in South Africa and England, he has seemed to become almost petulant, like some moody prince, when he has momentarily lost his timing or been forced to play a maiden over Thus whereas his first Test 100 in Durban in 1970 was the most perfect exhibition you could wish to see – the 100 reached four balls after lunch on the first day after a glorious array of quick-footed strokes – the second in Port

Elizabeth was very much of two parts. Having reached 50-odd with reasonable circumspection and attention to detail, he was pinned down for a few overs and thereafter slogged his way to 126, spectacularly and brilliantly but not always with what the purist would consider a proper adjustment of the feet.

In Australia, however, he has had a different success. It is part of the Australian outlook that if you produce the goods and do something better than they do, you are all right. And Richards' feats for South Australia were soon being acknowledged far away from Adelaide. He batted there, too, in a different way. At home and in England when he was well in, he has been wont to become almost arrogant in his contempt for the bowling and to take reckless risks which often remove him from the scene much earlier than the watcher would like. In Australia he went on, not perhaps with care – he scarcely had time to be careful when making 325 in a day in Perth – but without the same indifference to danger.

Obviously when you are earning a dollar a run, you would not be human if you threw away easy chances of augmenting the income. But there is more to it than that. On English pitches and against English bowling it is less easy to take liberties. He finished up his Australian season by going in with a broken finger and sharing in a brisk stand which allowed South Australia to declare and win the final match and the Sheffield Shield. His prestige stands very high indeed in Australia.

Barry Richards was born on July 21, 1945, in Durban, where within a few months the hospitals and nursing-homes also sent forth Graeme Pollock, Mike Procter and Lee Irvine.

The Australians of 1957–58 vaguely remember an unusual Durban High School boy of 12 at the nets and thereafter the advance was inexorable, though there was always speculation about whether he or Procter from Hilton College would be the better player. In fact, Procter played for South Africa first in 1966–67 as a fast bowler and Richards, though making runs handsomely against the Australians in other matches, came no nearer to the Test

Barry Richards

side than twelfth man. It was a deliberate policy by the selectors to bring him on gradually and not to disturb more than necessary an experienced and successful side of quite remarkable team spirit. They could afford not to play him and it must have been a nice thought that he was in reserve but it goes down as one of the great pieces of selectorial self-denial.

By the start of 1970, after making thousands of runs in England, he must have been just about the best player never to have played in a Test match. This was rectified in Cape Town in January and I can remember one episode which illustrated the stature of South Africa's new opening batsman.

With my eminent colleague, John Woodcock, I had a long talk on the Sunday of the Test match with Hassan Howa, the ebullient president of the South African Coloured Board of Control. I was trying hard to make Mr Howa's statements accord with what I knew to be the facts when, in extolling the merits of his own Coloured cricketers, he said, 'We have a better player than young Richards.'

'But,' I said, 'we think he is one of the best players in the world.'

Mr Howa brushed this aside. 'He is not sound,' he said.

'Have you seen him?' I asked.

'Oh, no, I haven't seen him. I don't go to Newlands.'

This was too much. We may have been bemused by some of the political aspects of the discussion but we did know something about Barry Richards and this disparagement of rare talent was hard to bear in a cricket world full of efficiency and short of genius.

English cricket with its strained finances and part-amateur traditions may find it hard to understand a young man unashamedly in the game for the money. The young man, equally understandably, may think that if he is one of the best in the world in his field, he deserves to be paid as such. But, given the talent to make a deep impact on the game, he can also build a reputation which will do more for him in the long term than any amount of cash in the short term, and I do not doubt that Barry Richards, strangely diffident about himself and his future, will finish up by being remembered for much more than the tens of thousands of runs he has made.

*Like his contemporary fellow-Springboks, Barry Richards has had no opportunity to play Test cricket since the series against Australia in 1969–70. International cricket's loss has continued to be county cricket's gain. For eight seasons he has made effortless centuries in all the major competitions, forming of late probably the most exciting and effective opening partnership in the world with West Indian Gordon Greenidge for Hampshire. Sometimes seemingly 'undismissible', sometimes apparently bored by the mediocrity around him, Richards has for long exemplified the champion unstretched by the challenge of his peers.—Ed.*

# TONY LEWIS

## by John Arlott

*The Cricketer* July 1971

Tony Lewis is a cricketer who has suffered from his obvious merits. In 1955, while he was still at Neath Grammar School, some years before he went up to the University, he played his first match for Glamorgan – against Leicestershire – and was, he recalls with a wide smile, out for 0, lbw shouldering arms to a vast chinaman from Jack Walsh. Five years later – after his National Service – he went up to Cambridge, where he won cricket and rugby Blues as a freshman. Sir Leonard Hutton emerged from retirement to play for Colonel L. C. Stevens' XI in that season and came back from the match saying he had seen a batsman who – and he made no qualifications – 'will make a good one'. Surely enough he went on to captain Cambridge in his third year; to set a new Glamorgan record of 238 for the second wicket with Alan Jones in 1962; and to score 2198 runs at 41.47 in 1966. Yet he was not satisfied and those most enthusiastic about his future – and he has always stood in favour at Lord's – still believed that he had yet to show his best.

Now it is to be felt that he has reached his maturity; not simply as a batsman; not only as a cricketer, but as a rounded human being whose immediate point of impact is on cricket. As a young man he took his rugby seriously – and capably – as a full-back for Gloucester, Neath and Cambridge before a knee injury ended his playing days. At Cambridge he read history for two years but eventually took his degree in modern languages; he now reads history for pleasure. He writes as well as any currently active first-class cricketer with the exception of Peter Walker; he also covers rugby football for the Press, and during the past winter he broadcast a regular morning sound-radio programme on BBC Wales. He has a characteristically Welsh

Tony Lewis

feeling for music; a shrewd interest in antiques; and is a happily involved family man.

All these facets of thought and activity account for the feeling that, over many years, he did not always concentrate on his 'middle-distance' fielding or the building of a major innings so completely as a single-minded cricketer might have done. In return for what may be regarded as a late maturity, he now does not handicap himself by 'pressing' or taking the game over-seriously as the one-track cricketer might do.

His quality as a batsman lies in timing, balance, speed of sight, reaction and movement – directed by an instinct to attack. He drives in the classic manner through the covers; cuts with a minimum of risk and plays in the modern idiom – with or against the spin and from off stump or leg – round a wide arc of the leg side. His speed is apparent in his adjustment; he will set out as if to drive a spinner, sway back without hurry and cut him; or he will whip away a ball which has swung late into his pads when one less rapid in definition might merely have taken it on the pad or played a hasty defensive stroke.

His confidence, the realization that he was no longer a young man of promise but a grown cricketer of achievement, came in 1969 when Glamorgan, under his captaincy, won the Championship for the second time. The succession to the Glamorgan captaincy was not simply. Maurice Turnbull and Wilfred Wooller were autocrats, the men who created and maintained the high standard of fielding that is now part of the county's reputation. John Clay was a continuing, benign influence but this was essentially the period of licking Welsh cricket into shape. Once that was done Ossie Wheatley came, as if upon his historic cue, to introduce the preponderantly relaxed – if not permissive – and democratic atmosphere of the 'sixties.

Thus Tony Lewis inherited a team of dual character, of highly efficient outcricket and friendly dressing-room atmosphere. At first there is little doubt that modesty, if not self-doubt, led him into uncertainty, and affected his batting; only the season before he had scored over two thousand runs; now he fell away. He does not hesitate to acknowledge the differing natures of the help he received; that Wilf Wooller stirred the rugby-style aggression in him; that Ossie Wheatley, still available from time to time to play and often to be convivial, confirmed him in friendly feeling with the side; that Don Shepherd instilled in him what he believed to be the key to captaincy – 'never change for the sake of change nor merely because the game seems tight and unmoving: never relax the pressure'; that Eifion Jones – 'you must always lean on the wicketkeeper to know what exactly is going on' – keeps him briefed; that Peter Walker often produced the side-of-mouth, wryly humorous remark that eased tension or anxiety.

He has been able to accept and assimilate all these influences because he has a lively all-round mind and a true sense of humour.

As he has grown to combine consistent batting with captaincy he has also moved from the mid-on, mid-off regions of the field to gully; has grown increasingly perceptive of the weaknesses of opponents and – though courteously – ruthless in the direction of his team in the field.

No Glamorgan captain has yet led an England team, though Maurice Turnbull could well have done, Wilfred Wooller should certainly have taken the 1950–51 team to Australia, and Lewis himself captained the MCC team to Asia in 1969–70. His appointment to captain the near-England-strength MCC team against the touring side indicates that interest in him remains favourable at Lord's. A century for Glamorgan and then a score of 87 – when he might have scored a second hundred if he had not been bustling for a declaration – were preliminary to top score in the first MCC innings against the Pakistanis and an enterprising declaration. If previously he had not lived up to trial opportunities, this looked like full acceptance.

An alert, dark-eyed and engaging character, Tony Lewis has much to commend him on several levels; he has not lost the urge to hit the ball over the top of the field; but he suppresses it at the need of his team. He leads a side perceptively and intelligently; and takes cricket as it happens. Six years younger than Illingworth, he seems his automatic successor; importantly, too, he is neither impatient for the honour nor even confident of gaining it. One of the advantages of a Welsh chapel upbringing is an ingrained knowledge of the Sermon on the Mount.

*Tony Lewis was eventually called upon to lead England. The opportunity arose at the end of the 1972 season, when Illingworth declared himself unavailable for the tour of the East. Lewis thus led England in his maiden Test, making 0 and 70 not out at Delhi in a match won by England by six wickets. He failed in the second and third, both lost, but made 125 in the drawn Kanpur match. He had scores of 74 and 88 during the three drawn Tests in Pakistan, but failed in the first home Test against New Zealand in 1973, and appeared in no further Test matches. Recurring injury and the desire to broaden his journalistic involvement in cricket and rugby prompted him to retire at the end of the 1974 season.—Ed.*

# MAJID KHAN

## by Mike Stevenson

*The Cricketer* August 1971

Shafqat Rana, who made his debut in Test cricket with his friend Majid, is a most cheerful character who regularly does his share of dressing-room clowning. Sometimes after some particularly extravagant comment on the subject of girls, cricket or whatever, he will catch Majid's eye.

'Shafqat,' Majid will say half-seriously, 'you are talking rubbish again. Don't forget there is one up there who hears everything.'

Majid Khan, whom Shafqat (and many more the world over besides!) rates among the ten best batsmen playing, is living proof of the fact that heredity in cricketers can be as crucial as it can in racehorses. Dr Jahangir Khan, his father, formerly Director of Education for the Government of West Pakistan and a lecturer in history at Punjab University, was a famous fast bowler for Cambridge and India in the 'thirties.

Even if he did not coach Majid a great deal, he clearly implanted in him love of the game, in addition to providing him with a rugged independence, tranquillity of temperament and maturity of character which have influenced his approach to sport as much as to life. It is symptomatic of Dr Jahangir Khan's attitude, both to parental and sporting problems, that when Majid was first selected to represent Pakistan, he resigned as a Test selector, because, in Majid's words: 'Quite apart from being suspected of favouritism, I'm sure he felt that if I failed he would be blamed.'

He was primarily a bowler initially and dismissed Lawry twice and Booth, all with bouncers, in his first Test; Shafqat said of his bouncer in those days: 'It was really nasty. Quick and coming straight at your eyes.' Doubts as to the legality of his basic delivery combined with a nasty back injury to influence Majid away from bowling towards batting and by 1965 he was back in the national side as a batsman.

After the great success during 1969 against the England Under-25 side in Pakistan he was, during the same year, their outstanding batsman in England if one excludes the Tests, where he was unable to reveal his real form.

In 1968 he joined Glamorgan and along with Len Muncer is one of the few non-Welshman to be taken to the hearts of the cricket-lovers of South Wales. Wilf Wooller, the Glamorgan county secretary and a great judge of the game, writes: 'A valuable trait in Majid's character is his calm approach to any problem in the middle. He has no use for dressing-room chat, which seems to invest this bowler or that with supernatural powers. He believes the ball should be met with the shot that it merits and this attitude has certainly helped to steady some of the Glamorgan players, especially the younger ones. I've always maintained that 50% of cricket is played in the mind and Majid is one of the players who has got just the right sort of mind!'

This basic calmness has even influenced the technique of his batting. He is so relaxed as a player that he seems to dig the ball out far later than most and thereby can create an impression of being basically a bottom-handed player. But his top hand is superbly in control when on the front foot and the certainty and variety of his strokeplay assure the fact that he is an exceptionally hard batsman at whom to bowl. In addition he has always been a great fighter, a fact well illustrated by the 111 that he scored in the second innings of his first first-class match, when Lahore were in danger of being thoroughly thrashed.

To adapt Voltaire's famous dictum, 'The man is the cricket.' Zakir Hussain, a journalist on the staff of the *New Times,* Rawalpindi, who is accompanying the Pakistan team on their present tour, was very interesting on this particular subject:

'Majid is a very pious man. He's a non-smoker and non-drinker. I remember when he was selected again for Pakistan (after being dropped) and to celebrate he took a number of his friends, myself included, to an ice-cream party! He is

Majid Khan

not fanatically orthodox Muslim but more what you would call a humanist.'

Perhaps the nearest approximation to an Achilles heel that Majid possesses is the fact that (like the character in Damon Runyon who 'dearly loved to commit eating') he is a highly dedicated trencherman.

Pervez Sajjad, the slow left-hander and another of Majid's many friends, tells of an incident that illustrates his talents in this department:

'During the Eaglets tour we were arriving in Ashby-de-la-Zouch too late to get anything at a restaurant; as there were six or seven of us we ordered 36 rounds of sandwiches, thinking that this meant 36 pieces of bread and not 72! About an hour and a half later the waiter arrived with two trays full and we got started on them but could only eat about half. So we rang Boku's room (Boku is the Punjabi nickname Majid has acquired, which roughly approximates to our own 'bucket-hands') and he came down and polished off the lot without any trouble at all!'

And now to add to his other triumphs, Majid has conquered Cambridge. I had the good luck and privilege to play for the University for four years in the early 'fifties and am, I suppose, as aware as most of the problems facing a university captain. All four captains under whom I played were Test players and all found it hard, even when there was a generally higher standard of cricket at Oxford and Cambridge than there is today, to bridge the gap between the Test players and the ordinary mortals!

Majid, by means of encouragement, coaching and superb captaincy on the field, has overcome this problem triumphantly.

With this achievement in mind, it seems to me appropriate to allow the last word on Majid to Cyril Coote, groundsman and cricketing sage at Fenner's since 1936:

'When Cambridge beat Pakistan early in the season, there was a time when Asif was belting the Varsity bowlers all over Fenner's. Majid bowled off-spinners off a couple of paces, got someone to do the same at the other end and he just managed one over with the new ball before lunch. Asif was caught behind and I wondered then how many captains on the county circuit would have done the same. I reckon he's the best captain we've had at Cambridge in my time.'

*Majid Khan, appointed captain in 1973, finished top of Glamorgan's batting averages in 1975, as he had in the three previous seasons, and continued to play memorable innings at several levels of competition. In 1974 he reached a century inside 28 overs for Pakistan against England in a one-day international at Trent Bridge; in 1975 he (213) and Shafiq Ahmed put on a record 389 for Punjab's first wicket against Sind; later that year, in a John Player League match at Wellingborough, he made 75 in 27 minutes. He played for Queensland in 1973–74, and captained Pakistan in three Test matches against England in 1973.—Ed.*

# BASIL D'OLIVEIRA

## by Mike Stevenson

*The Cricketer* September 1971


'Rags to Riches' is a theme sufficiently well documented in the realms of pantomime to have acquired an outsize aura of unreality. Though more laboured, 'Subservience to Dignity' (if one is searching for a tag) aptly describes the extraordinary career of Basil Lewis D'Oliveira.

Having scraped into appointment as a league professional in 1960, his progress has been meteoric; he is established as a front-line, middle-order Test batsman, is financially secure and is regarded, by almost all whose view is not tinged with a sprinkling of jealousy, with respect, admiration and often affection.

Each major hurdle that has confronted him has been met with the same essential resolution and steadfast, enquiring empiricism that has assured the gradual emergence of the mature Test player out of the embryonically optimistic smiter who scored, on the Cape matting, at a speed that makes the more predatory exploits of Garfield Sobers or Clive Lloyd appear positively pedestrian.

But in order fully to understand the mature concert artist it is necessary to examine his 'honky-tonk' origins. Facilities for non-white cricketers in South Africa have improved in recent years but when D'Oliveira was starting his career they were appalling. The game was played on matting and even the fastest bowling was often faced without gloves, box or sometimes even pads.

The bowler tried his damnedest to smash the middle stump and the batsman tried to hit him for six!

It was against a backdrop of this sort of cricket that Peter Walker, whose memory appears to have deteriorated more markedly than his close fielding, conjectures whether or not it was 1959 in which he helped to organize what he

74

Basil D'Oliveira

believes to be the first multi-racial cricket match in South Africa.

It was held at the 'Natalspruit', the only non-European cricket ground in Johannesburg, and was played between an XI comprised of Indians, Cape Coloureds and one African, which was called 'The South African Selected Non-European XI'; the team for which Peter Walker played was composed of English cricketers coaching in South Africa plus a few Springboks.

D'Oliveira played for, and captained, the non-European side, failing in the first innings but scoring an impressive 40 in the second. When Peter Walker was phoned by Middleton Cricket Club and asked to give his opinion on D'Oliveira's ability and potential, he had no hesitation in recommending him.

During the match, the whites and non-whites changed in separate dressing-rooms and ate separately; but one of the English players suggested that it would be a good thing to 'get together' with the opposition. Peter Walker's creditable reaction was to drive to an off-licence, fill his cricket bag with grog and, after the departure of the special branch police, who had been on duty at the match, organize the traditional 'entertainment of the opposition', which is taken for granted in this country but was an unsettling innovation to D'Oliveira and his colleagues.

Basil's reaction to the invitation was understandably cautious. 'Do you think it'll be all right, Mr Walker?' But suspicion soon changed to pleasurable surprise that they should be so treated and, Walker said to me, 'I got the impression that a number of the non-white side were genuinely moved. I reckon that in a matter of minutes we had created an atmosphere which was unique in South Africa.'

D'Oliveira's chance to advance in cricket occurred in 1960; an article in *World Sports* had trumpeted his prowess and listed, among his most remarkable feats: 80 centuries in South African Cape cricket, 46 runs off one 8-ball over, and an innings of 225 scored, incredibly, in 70 minutes.

News of his accomplishments, moreover, had filtered back to England after he had played against a number of established cricketers in Rhodesia and, after Middleton Cricket Club in the Central Lancashire League had been unable to agree terms with Wes Hall, they offered D'Oliveira £450, out of which he was expected to find his air fare of £200.

He accepted with alacrity and the story of how he watched, learnt and said nothing during a nightmarish few weeks before his first runs came is told with disarming candour in his autobiography, simply entitled *D'Oliveira*. He is unstinting in his gratitude to the league cricketers of Lancashire, and among them John Kay, the cricket-writer (instrumental in his appointment at Middleton), who met him on his arrival in London. 'I was impressed at once with his sincerity. I've never met a man more desperately anxious to succeed.'

Success came fast and he finished the season ahead of Sobers at the top of the Central Lancashire League averages. The flower-strewn path he travelled, via Commonwealth tours, through county cricket into the Test arena is also well-known, as is his debt to Tom Graveney.

What of the 'D'Oliveira method'? As a batsman he is admirably 'sideways-on', employing a very short backlift, which still provides his powerful forearms with sufficient purchase to hit the ball with immense power. He is watchful for the opening stages of an innings, allowing the bowler an apparent dominance that will be gradually wrested from him. This, of course, is why he has acquired the reputation for being a poor starter; above all, character and concentration are the keynotes to his play, which appears to me to have been far more consistently successful than players endowed with even more natural talent than he possesses.

As a bowler, he can really swing the ball as well as make it 'wobble' disconcertingly and has developed the reputation of a formidable stand breaker.

What of his politics? It is naïve, I think, to presume that his willingness to play with and against South Africans bespeaks any tacit approval of apartheid. My own guess is that as an essentially simple man he wishes to confine his life and activities to spheres with which he is familiar. If he plays in a match with a South African who scores one run– he must score two. If the 'enemy' gets one wicket– he must get two.

It is also my opinion that he has been well-advised to keep his mouth firmly closed on controversial issues and get on with his cricket.

He serves first-class cricket in one other way. Since the retirement of a certain jovial antipodean who played for Somerset, his mantle has descended firmly on Basil's shoulders, all and sundry finding endless pleasure from attempting to guess or discover his correct date of birth.

*For some time after he had played the last of his 48 Tests many felt that Basil D'Oliveira might have been a very useful member of the England XI. In 1975, when apparently he was approaching 44 years of age, he averaged 43 for Worcestershire without making a century. His extremely successful benefit that year was a measure of his popularity in the county and elsewhere. Future generations, of course, will associate his name with far more then superb all-round cricketing ability and sportsmanship.—Ed.*

# MIKE DENNESS

## by Tony Pawson

*The Cricketer* January 1972

For a Scotsman to captain a county and play for England is a unique achievement. Apart from Mike Denness, only one other Scottish-born county captain (in later years), Ian Peebles, has ever been included in an England Test team. It is appropriate that this pair should also be those rarities of the modern game – an attacking batsman and a spin bowler.

Of Ian Peebles, Sir Donald Bradman wrote, 'I had the frustrating experience of meeting a slow googly bowler whose delivery presented a hazard I had not previously encountered as I could not detect his googly from his leg-break. This would have been bad enough had the perpetrator of my discomfort been a fellow Australian, or an Englishman, but he was a Scot.'

Mike Denness has not yet reached that Test stature – or indeed played against the Australians. But his ability was well summed up by K. N. Prabhu, who wrote in our *Winter Annual* that the Indian team rated him the finest batsman they encountered over here and were relieved that he did not catch the selectors' eye.

A delightful strokemaker, an enthusiastic and perceptive captain, and a fine fielder close to the wicket or in the covers, Denness is always a joy to watch.

Englishmen, of course, have a profound ignorance of Scottish cricket and tend to regard the Scot who plays the game well as something of a freak. Like Dr Johnson's talking dog, he is not expected to perform well; the wonder is that he should perform at all.

This attitude was well-illustrated the first time Denness made runs for Kent. A distinguished commentator rushed round to the dressing room and unfortunately picked on that inveterate leg-puller, Peter Richardson, to fill him in on Mike's background. So the writing world heard, as it no doubt expected to hear, that Denness was the son of a poor Banffshire sheep-farmer and his unusual passion for the game had involved him in a hundred-mile bicycle ride every time he wanted a match. At lunch the discomforted commentator was given the true facts – that his father had been an enthusiastic cricketer and that Mike had lived for many years in a house adjoining the pavilion at Ayr, one of Scotland's leading cricket clubs.

In his early teens Mike Denness benefited from the coaching of Charlie Oakes, the Sussex player who had become Ayr's first professional. The standard of club cricket in that area was as good as in an English county and this too helped to develop his game.

Rugby then was an equal love. At school Denness played in representative sides with Ian McLaughlin, later to be the Scottish international forward, and Ian Ure, that renegade to first-division soccer. At that stage Mike was better than either, playing for a representative Glasgow Schoolboys' side and even having a trial for Glasgow and District seniors.

Denness was so successful with Ayr that he was recommended to E. W. Swanton as a potential county player. His first thoughts were of Warwickshire, but a fellow Scot, J. M. Allan, was then playing for Kent and persuaded him to try for that county. Denness was keen to play first-class cricket, but he delayed moving south until he found a job giving security in winter.

Then in July 1962 he had his first game in the Kent side as an amateur. His debut was at Dover and it was hardly the kindest of introductions. Batting against Essex on a fierce 'turner' he had to face Jim Laker, the game's deadliest destroyer on a spinners' wicket. In two innings he contrived only three runs and faced no other bowler.

His next match was against Surrey and the situation was hardly calculated to restore his confidence. The score was 26 for 4 when he went in to bat and at once Peter Loader knocked his cap off with the first bouncer he had ever seen. That was a test of nerve in which he proved himself with a courageous fifty.

Mike Denness

Denness had for long been an avid student of the game, watching players on television and trying to model himself on Graveney, May and Cowdrey. Now he had Cowdrey to coach and advise him.

He recalls with gratitude the value of those lessons. In one early innings, a slow left-hander was bowling on his off stump to a packed off-side field. For a couple of overs he drove him into the covers without beating the fielders. Then Cowdrey came down the wicket and advised taking a leg-stump guard to give himself more room for his shot. At once he could steer his strokes through the narrow gaps.

He remained a middle-order batsman until Cowdrey suddenly asked him to open against Yorkshire at Bradford, giving him no time for worry. Soon he found he enjoyed this, for his weakness then was against slow bowling, which he played firm-footed from the crease. With the confidence of runs in the book against the faster bowlers, it was easier to use his feet.

Now he has become a good player of spin bowlers. Even on bad wickets he attacks them, aiming to disrupt their control of length and line. His power is in the drive and he always hits with the spin, uninfluenced by Alan Knott's uniquely successful style of sweeping against the turn on the half-volley.

It is Brian Luckhurst who has had the strongest effect on his batting for they soon developed into a formidable opening pair, ideally balanced. Luckhurst's patient reliability gives Denness freedom to play his own strokes with flair and flourish. He likes to start quietly, getting the feel and the pace of the pitch. Once his eye is in he accepts more risks in going for his shots.

This formula for success was disastrously abandoned in his first Test innings. Against New Zealand at The Oval in 1969 he found the bowlers so accurate in line and length that nothing was given away. It took him 47 minutes to score and he was in nearly an hour for 2. Analysing his failure he realized the occasion had been so important for him that he had hesitated too long to take any chance. In the second innings he had the courage to play his normal game, scoring an attractive fifty.

82

He played against the Rest of the World the following year, but his own and England's failure on a green Lord's wicket cost him his place.

He does not, however, regard himself as having played in Tests. For he feels that four matches is the minimum in which to show oneself and the selectors whether one has the temperament and ability for Test match cricket.

In county cricket he has been consistently successful without any peaks of brilliance. He scored 1000 runs in his second season and every season thereafter.

The highlight of his career was Kent's first Gillette Cup win. Denness gave the innings a racing start with drives of grace and power which threatened to destroy Somerset. Though the Kent innings fell apart later, this was enough to win his county the trophy and himself the Man of the Match award.

Denness has always been nimble between the wickets and has a fine understanding with Luckhurst. Some find Luckhurst's running difficult to interpret for he has a habit of starting down the wicket without calling or intending to run. But Denness has always regarded it as a basic principle that the non-striker should call as well as the striker – even for strokes in front of the wicket – and this prevents misunderstanding.

Next season may well be vital to his career. At 30 he has not long to go if he is to make an impact as a Test cricketer. What more challenging opportunity can there be than an Australian tour?

*Controversy – volumes of it – was awaiting Mike Denness. Illingworth was dropped at the end of the 1973 series and Denness was chosen to lead England in West Indies that winter. Losing the first Test and valiantly achieving draws in the next two, his side went to Trinidad for the fifth Test after rain had spoilt the fourth, and Boycott's batting and Greig's bowling pulled off a sensational victory. Denness not only retained the captaincy at this eleventh hour, but proceeded to make two centuries in the three home Tests against India. Failure in the three Tests against Pakistan failed to ruffle the selectors, who appointed him to lead MCC in Australia and New Zealand in 1974–75. By the fourth Test he felt it necessary to drop himself from the side after continual failure against Australia's pace attack, but a half-century in the Adelaide Test preceded an astonishing 188 in the final Test, at Melbourne, when Thomson was absent and Lillee broke down. England won by an innings (to finish four-one down), and Denness's score was the highest ever by an England captain in a Test in Australia. At Auckland a fortnight later he made 181 against New Zealand. The topsy-turvy Denness era ended dismally at Edgbaston when he put Australia in to bat and England lost by an innings. He failed to reach double-figures in either innings, was dropped from the side and the captaincy was given to Tony Greig for the remainder of the series.—Ed.*

# LANCE GIBBS

## by M. J. K. Smith

*The Cricketer* February 1972

Lance Gibbs is yet another top-class performer who changed horses in mid-stream. He was originally a leg-spinner, until, as he tells it, he met Robert Christiani in a Guyana trial. Christiani gave him so much stick he convinced him there had to be a better way; and so he turned to off-spinning. Quite obviously he will go down as one of the game's great performers in this style.

He has 209 Test wickets, which is the highest number taken by any West Indian, and also the highest by any off-spinner – followed by Jim Laker with 193. He had a hat-trick v. Australia at Adelaide on the 1960–61 tour, after taking three wickets in four balls in the previous Test.

Against India at Bridgetown on the 1962 tour his figures were 53.3–37–38–8. The list is endless, but those examples are enough to underline his class. He made his debut for Guyana against MCC in 1953–54 when Willie Watson (257) and Tom Graveney (231) shared a stand of 402. It would have been difficult to find a better player of off-spinners than Graveney to start against.

Gibbs tells an amusing story against himself from the same game, when Godfrey Evans talked him into having a go at hitting Johnny Wardle out of the ground . . . Gibbs stumped Evans bowled Wardle.

By the close of the 1971 season Lance Gibbs had taken 804 wickets in first-class cricket at an average of 26.19.

He made his Test debut in 1957–58. Three times he has toured England, with the successful West Indian sides of 1963 and 1966, and as vice-captain of the 1969 side.

A natural, Gibbs developed a technique all his own. It goes without saying that performers of this class have accuracy and control, to which he allies tremendous spin from a high arm action, which gives him bounce, and a lot of variation in pace from slow to medium-fast.

The interesting feature of his technique is his method of delivery. The majority of bowlers must deliver against some resistance, i.e. the braced left side (for right-handers). Lance bowls 'in his run' and gets his spin from a very supple wrist and long fingers. If you meet him, have a look at the lower joint on his spinning finger, the right index, which looks as though someone has flattened it out with a hammer. This deformity has been caused by the amount of spin he imparts.

Few can get a boy's ball into this position in the hand, let alone a big one, and this enables him really to wrap the index finger around the ball and spin it like a top.

Since he is 'in his run' on delivery he has a definite advantage in getting into the field, and it is difficult to envisage anyone covering more ground off his own bowling. On more than one occasion I have seen him bowl over the wicket to a left-hander and field the attempted short singles into the covers on the other side of the wicket. In short he is an extra man in the field and one who has always had more than his share of run-outs.

Already successful throughout the world, he qualified for Warwickshire and to everyone's surprise met with relatively little success in county cricket. He had his days, as against Glamorgan in 1970 when he returned the season's and his career-best figures of 8 for 37, but it wasn't until last season, 1971, that he really went to town. Then he made a few pay for the liberties they had taken previously.

Why did he struggle? Undoubtedly he had played an awful lot of cricket and was often starting the season tired. Also, as he will say, it took him some considerable time to sort out the particular problems of county as opposed to Test cricket. Basically he had not often been asked to perform on the variety of wickets found in county cricket, and in particular the wet ones and turners, where one would have thought he would excel. Now he does excel because he will happily bowl round the wicket as well as he does over.

Previously he hadn't fancied going round and it took him a long time to accept the necessity of this under these conditions. This particular problem was accentuated by

Lance Gibbs

his line, which was basically from the edge of the crease across the batsman. The majority of English bowlers try and get as close to the wickets as possible on delivery, so that their line is wicket-to-wicket.

Fred Titmus is a prime example of this among off-spinners. This gives them a better chance of an lbw decision and forces the batsman to play the ball more often than someone bowling from wide. Lance, generally pitching well outside the off stump, was padded off *ad nauseam* in his first seasons. Or else the front leg went down the wicket and the sweep was played – the obvious moves to counter this are to bowl a straighter line or to go round the wicket, at this time his two relative weaknesses.

His success this year did, of course, coincide with the lbw intent clause, which cut out a lot of padding off; but I doubt that was half as important as going round the wicket when it turned enough. Then, with his bounce and spin, everyone was in trouble. His figures certainly didn't flatter him and they speak for themselves . . . 131 wickets at 18.89 from 1024 overs, a striking rate of a wicket every seven to eight overs, which is very high.

His approach is typically West Indian, active and aggressive while retaining and exhibiting that enjoyment of the game and pride of performance which makes them such an attraction. In the field he is very quick onto the ball, and a fine close catcher, particularly at gully.

Gibbs' skills are confined to bowling and fielding and he can lay no claim to be an all-rounder. He has yet to score a fifty in a first-class match and has never got beyond 43.

Perhaps it would have been more interesting if he were to describe his own batting, which skippers consistently assign to No. 11. To give himself the required room to swing, the left leg is usually placed well away from the line of the ball, and the off-side slash essayed in various guises. However, he is quite capable of propping up for another batsman, and in particular of scampering up the wicket to give him the strike or to get away from someone he doesn't fancy. So this aspect of his game may be considered interesting but erratic.

L. R. Gibbs was born on September 29, 1934 and made

his debut in Tests at 23, playing in four of the five matches against Pakistan in West Indies.

The recent decline in West Indies Test performances has coincided with his diminished success. But at 37 he is still a most accomplished bowler, as he proved again last season.

Off the field he has a keen interest in the horses, and, to pinch a phrase, this one is certainly a thoroughbred.

*Lance Gibbs, having bowled more than 25,000 balls in Test cricket – many more than anyone else in history – passed 300 wickets in Tests during West Indies' series in Australia in 1975–76. Going on to pass Fred Trueman's record of 307, it remained to be seen how far he could stretch the new figure before retirement after a long and honourable career.—Ed.*

# GRAHAM McKENZIE

## by Gerard Dent

*The Cricketer* March 1972

Generally speaking easy-going people do not reach the top of their professions. Graham Douglas McKenzie is a very remarkable exception. Even more remarkably for an easy-going Australian, he has stayed there.

Slow to smile and slow to speak, he burst upon the world of cricket like a thunderclap. In his Test debut at Lord's in 1961, on his twentieth birthday, his 34 runs of the 102 added by the last two wickets were a vital contribution to Australia's lead of 134 in the first innings. Then, bowling with rare pace and power on the notorious Lord's ridge, he took five wickets for 37 runs, including those of Dexter and May, to send England plummeting to destruction.

A few weeks later his influence on the Old Trafford Test was hardly less crucial. That match, which he considers to be the greatest game of cricket in which he ever played, is chiefly remembered for its climax, for the bravura of Dexter and the deadly spin of Benaud; but the stage had already been set.

When, as last man, McKenzie came in to join Davidson, Australia, only 157 ahead, were facing defeat. The 32 runs he made were priceless as he held on while his partner flayed away at the other end to add 98 between them.

That victory made Australia two-one in the series, and with only the Oval Test to come the Ashes were retained.

A few months earlier Jack Ryder had made a journey of 4000 miles to Perth and back. As one of the selectors he recognised that there was at that time a yawning gap in Australian cricket. With Lindwall, Miller and Johnston becoming distant memories, the heat and burden of the late 'fifties had been borne by Davidson at one end, while the other was occupied by a variety of bowlers some of whose actions would have given Syd Buller nightmares.

Graham McKenzie

By the season of 1960–61 Don Bradman and his co-selectors had become very exercised on the subject of throwing. Though Meckiff was not finally drummed out until 1963, the saga of the South African Griffin had reached its climax at Lord's the previous June. Consequently anyone with untoward kinks in his action was looked upon with the greatest suspicion.

Graham McKenzie had one of the straightest arms in cricket. With his beautiful, smooth and powerful action and his unusual pace off the wicket, it was only his inexperience that held him back. After his second first-class match in early 1960 his State captain Ken Meuleman said 'McKenzie will never be a batsman, but as bowler he will be a sensation!'

He could not have timed his arrival better. His third first-class game was against none other then Frank Worrell's record-breaking West Indians at the start of their 1960–61 tour. His 4 for 41 for Western Australia in the second innings was not forgotten.

Hence the 4000-mile round trip by Mr Ryder, and England for McKenzie. Certainly few if any selectors had had any reason to make that trip before. One thousand five hundred miles of Nullarbor Plain had effectively divided the West from the East, and it was not until 1956–57 that the West Australians took a full part in the Sheffield Shield competition.

Born in Cottesloe, a quiet seaside suburb of Perth, Graham McKenzie grew up in an atmosphere largely unaffected by the world outside. But with two cricket fanatics in the family, his uncle and his father, he did not lack for encouragement.

For most of his early cricketing life he was a batsman and an occasional spin bowler. It was not until 1958–59 that he tried his hand at bowling seamers. 'I suddenly realised that it was my strength and there was no looking back now.' There was none indeed. Fifty wickets, average 14.5, in second grade that season and 49, average 11.21, in first grade in the next, and by early 1960 he was in the State side.

Since his sensational Test debut he has brought under control his immense physical powers. His run-up is economical in length and with 14½st in weight and over 6ft in height behind every delivery he is an intimidating opponent. At his fastest he cuts the ball off the wicket like a whiplash. His batting, alternately languid and lusty, has made many significant contributions, including 76 against South Africa at Sydney in 1963–64.

For ten years now he has been an integral part of the Australian Test team, the first West Australian to be so, and during those years has passed nearly every statistical milestone. On his second tour of England in 1964 he equalled Grimmett's record for an Australian in England in taking 29 Test wickets. This achievement formed part of an even greater one. Between December 1963 and December 1964 he took no fewer than 73 Test wickets, 16 in Australia against South Africa, 29 in England, 21 in India and Pakistan, and seven more against the Pakistanis on their way to tour New Zealand.

During this glut of wicket-taking he became the youngest cricketer ever to take 100 wickets in Test cricket – Valentine took 139 days longer.

He was the youngest to the 200 also, four years later against West Indies at Melbourne in the match in which he achieved his best Test performance of 8 for 71. But his career has had its undulations. He was dropped against England for the fourth Test in 1965–66, though in the event he performed very successfully as a last-minute replacement. He was the only effective bowler in his country's humiliation in South Africa in 1966–67, and then suffered humiliation himself in England in 1968 and in South Africa in 1969–70.

After three years' hard work in English county cricket with Leicestershire and some intermittent success in Rest of the World teams he is far and away the most experienced bowler Australia has got. He is also the most prolific.

Not yet 31, he himself feels that though some of his prowess has been blunted by the unsympathetic nature of the Grace Road pitches, he is performing as well as ever. His 4 for 66 in the Perth match against the Rest of the World should not be lost among the adulations heaped on Massie and Lillee.

With a temperament which, unlike most bowlers', remains unruffled by changes and chances, Garth, as he is nicknamed, has it in him to influence events as much as he ever has in the past.

*The Australian selectors were never again to call up Graham McKenzie, and his total of 246 Test wickets remains second to Benaud's 248. He was still a considerable bowler in 1975, though his 32 wickets for the county champions, Leicestershire, cost 33 apiece. This most popular and reliable of cricketers announced his retirement at the end of that season.—Ed.*

# GEOFFREY BOYCOTT

## by Mike Stevenson

*The Cricketer* April 1972

However entrancingly captivating the demeanour of a kitten may be, its triple round of eating, sleeping and play is instinctively dedicated (with natural fanaticism) to a clearly-defined end. 'How sweet,' say the children as it darts, sidles and skips its way through a hundred crazy variants of feline choreography. 'How gentle.'

Yet the little animal is learning how to kill. Survival demands (or demanded before the advent of tinned cat-food) that footwork, co-ordination, judgment, speed and concentration should be just so.

Geoffrey Boycott, arguably one of the best three batsmen playing today, has much in common with that kitten. The flame of his personality has been fanned by ambition to a white-hot point of single-mindedness, dedicated to success. He has trained himself by observation, study and practice – to kill – and the fact that his victims are bowlers and not mice does not disrupt the analogy.

He was born (like so many other fine cricketers) of mining stock at Fitzwilliam, near Pontefract, on October 21, 1940, and youthful performances of great promise prompted a benevolent uncle to launch a family fund designed to send Geoffrey to Johnny Lawrence's indoor cricket school at Rothwell. Apart from the actual coaching in technique that he received Boycott was fortunate to have regular opportunity of practice against leg-spin and googly bowling, a style of attack that, skilfully purveyed, seems normally able to establish a relationship with most Yorkshire batsmen reminiscent of a mongoose with a snake.

Advancement came speedily both at school and club level until, in his early teens, he experienced success in Yorkshire Council and Yorkshire League cricket. Reasonably well-authenticated rumour has it that his troubles over running and calling started in these formative years and that, after playing a number of matches for Barnsley, certain more mature colleagues in the side were not exactly enamoured of the prospect of batting with him.

A move to the Leeds club following invitation by Billy Sutcliffe was the prelude to meteoric advancement and if, as his light step took him up these foothills, the dejected figures of the run-outs were quickly forgotten it was surely at this stage a venial sin. He headed the Yorkshire Colts' averages after his first season and the following year, 1962, played four matches for the county. His talent was obvious as, unfortunately, was his potential as a wicket-taker, the victims normally being members of his own side.

Without attempting to adjudicate over apportionment of blame, the fact is that two run-outs in his first two games for Yorkshire elicited such a storm of disapproval that rebuke from captain and certain colleagues was both swift and, sadly, far from private. This, in my view at least, was the time when crucial lessons might have been learnt. Instead the cat licked its wounds, strengthened its resolve to be 'Top Cat' and continued its lonely journey. There was no time now for play. Success and survival were all that mattered.

As a batsman the ripening process was both admirable and continuous. Boycott is and was the most assiduous practiser (did he not give his notice as a wages clerk some time before he need have done in order to be able to precede the 1964 season with four different sessions of net practice each day?). A hint of frailty outside the off stump, a tendency to drop the hands too near to the ground on the forward stroke and a short period when his initial movement, prior to the ball's delivery, of the right foot back and across seemed to inhibit him in effective play off his leg stump, all became things of the past. Here was a gladiator. Someone was going to suffer.

Like Sutcliffe and Hutton before him, outstanding ability had been allied to the eradication of error, the result being as evident statistically as it must have been in terms of perspiration expended by suffering bowlers. His attitude to life and to the game that was his life was also

Geoffrey Boycott

apparent in the remarkable and praiseworthy improvement that occurred in the standard of his fielding. As runs began to flow more and more freely, so spectacles were discarded for contact lenses and, in his own view, an increase in social confidence resulted. His signature as a world-famous sportsman on the contract of a well-known agency followed logically. Boycott was in business.

With every airing on television or radio, Geoff Boycott's image improved in the eyes of the uninitiated but to those engaged in first-class cricket in whatever capacity the interviews seemed to bear little relationship to reality. However free the flow of runs from his bat, the sad fact remained that joy was lacking and it still appeared to be certain that the old cliché that the game is greater than the player had not been learned.

Suddenly the unanticipated occurred. Close departed into exile and Boycott was Yorkshire's new captain. The cat had been asked to become a lion. The pride of cricketers in his charge was far less successful than their leader, who became the first batsman to end an English Championship season with a three-figure average; but sadly few batting bonus points were acquired in the process. Moreover his declaration in the match against Northants at Harrogate (apparently dictated by calculation of the computers in 'Boycott House' that subsequent dismissal would bring his average back into the 90s) certainly assured the record but it did not seem to fit convincingly into the context of the game.

To those people who might have expected a factual and statistical examination of Boycott's undoubted stature as a batsman, may I say that I am paradoxically attempting to pay him a compliment. The charge of ruthless selfishness is there. It will not go away if he turns his back and pretends that it does not exist. A large number of cricketers and journalists appear to have written him off as incapable of improving his attitude.

I am not among them. I hope that Geoffrey Boycott will be remembered for more than an indigestible mass of statistics, however impressive.

Cricket should be a game of joy. Ideally it should be

played in the sunshine. There is still time to see the light and for the lion to emerge.

*No modern cricketer has been enveloped in so much controversy and attempted analysis as Geoff Boycott. After making 99 and 112 to help set up England's amazing victory at Port-of-Spain in 1974 he was inexplicably dismissed cheaply twice by India's innocuous-looking opening bowlers at Old Trafford, having scored a hundred in each innings of the early-season Test trial. He missed the rest of the 1974 Tests, was chosen for the Australian tour, and then stunned the cricket world by withdrawing shortly before departure, declaring that he had no wish to play for England. In 1975 he led his young Yorkshire team to second place in the County Championship.—Ed.*

# IAN CHAPPELL

## by Ray Robinson

*The Cricketer* May 1972

Englishmen will see Ian Chappell standing a little taller at the wicket than he did last time England's bowlers attacked him in Test matches.

As the tour of Britain begins, Australia's new captain stands correspondingly high in the estimation of his countrymen – almost as high as his run total in the recent Australian season: 1140 in 12 games, when nobody else reached 900.

Chappell's more erect posture is prompted neither by backache nor dreamed-up theory but is a practical response to an ex-captain's hint. Bob Simpson noticed that Ian had bowed into a stoop that put part of his head outside the off stump. Correcting this, a more upright stance brings his blue eyes level.

These adjustments required no running-in period. As the only player who made four centuries in the Rest of the World series, he wound up batting at his best. In nimble footwork to upset bowlers' length Chappell has few peers.

Whereas sons of great cricketers often feel at a loss living in the shadow of their sires – for instance Richard Hutton and John Bradsen (né Bradman) – chromosomes, genes and time have been kinder to grandsons of Victor Richardson, Australia's vice-captain in England in 1930 and captain touring South Africa in 1935. Ian, Gregory and Trevor Chappell have inherited much of the ball sense that made their redoubtable grandsire South Australia's most versatile athlete. Their father, Martin Chappell, a leading baseballer, headed Adelaide's first-grade cricket scoring with 513 as an opening batsman in 1950–51, when Ian was seven, already the best player in the nursery.

After notable deeds at Prince Alfred College, Ian was chosen for South Australia at 18, so confident that at 19 he

100

Ian Chappell

made a century against Benaud and Davidson's bowling.

On his Test debut at 21 against Pakistan in Melbourne Chappell held four slip catches, though his interstate baseball mates thought it a pity that his powerful throwing arm was not given more scope farther from the wicket.

Now 28, Chappell enters the field with a toes-out walk unusual in agile men – Sir Leonard Hutton was another. This athletic South Australian is more substantial in build, standing 5ft 11in, and has almost 13 stone to put into his shots. Successor to Simpson at slip, he has brought off 53 catches in 37 Tests.

When he got to England at 24 in 1968 his fighting spirit was admired in a year when centuries were almost as scarce as good wickets. Only John Edrich (554) scored more runs than Ian's 348 in the five Tests.

Three Test series between mid-1968 and the end of 1969 obliged the Australians to cope with different styles of bowlers on dissimilar tracks – English, Australian and Indian. Exceptional footwork enabled Chappell to adapt his batting to the three changes resourcefully. When the Aussies moved on to the homeland of Richards and Pollock, captain Bill Lawry announced Chappell as 'the best batsman in the world – on all types of wickets'. Hardly as well-timed as the speaker's own sweep, this statement tempted Providence.

Providence neutrally abstained from having a part in the controversy. Chappell's adaptor blew a fuse and his highest score in four Tests in South Africa was 34. 'It was hard to produce your best in Africa after our Indian tour and I just went bad,' he put it, simply.

In Australia last year John Snow made the most of Chappell's habit of twisting rather square-on in back-foot defence, making it more difficult to evade bouncers rearing at his breastbone than a side-on posture does. Ian's 2219 runs in 37 Tests include six centuries and 10 fifties.

Ian was called to the captaincy last year, replacing Lawry at a time when the barometer was persistently set low for Australia: five losses in the nine preceding Tests, unrelieved by a single win. Not many Aussie skippers have got England out under 200 at first attempt, as Chappell did at

Sydney. In his deployment of bowlers and placings of fields there were touches recalling Benaud's first attempt against England at Brisbane 13 years earlier.

When a wicket fell near the end of his first day as captain he came in himself, with two minutes to go. If in such a situation it is some other batsman's turn, Ian consults him on whether he or a nightwatchman will go in. After the losing skipper in Sydney had seen his outplayed Australians off to their various States, he dropped in on the Englishmen's victory party to wish them well for the New Zealand trip and their flight home.

No avid student of Test history, Chappell plays the game as it comes. In the neutral opinion of Barry Richards, who played a season with South Australia: 'Chappell is an easy captain to play under. He gives every player a chance to use his own judgment, without making too many demands.'

The atmosphere in the Australian room is less charged with the tension that makes bowlers look harder to play. It is more as sportsmen's changing quarters ought to be, less like a courtroom awaiting the jury's return.

Never the soonest under the shower and the first to depart, Ian usually takes it easy with clusters of players relaxing over a few beers. Yarning over the day's happenings, relating them to relevant events, they get exasperations (if any) out of their systems.

As a result of the brothers' names being printed as Chappell, I. and Chappell, G., one nickname given Ian has been 'Chappelli', as if he came from Agropoli instead of Adelaide. In a city where cricket looms large Signor Chappelli's home number no longer appears in the telephone directory, to save the phone running hot in the evenings.

Though Chappell's sides lost the recent series to the World XI, 2–1, captain Garry Sobers acknowledged that the Australians played the better cricket and batted more attractively in scoring 4.2 runs an over to the World XI's 3.8 an over.

Ian's thumb is not yet hardened by pinning up batting orders. Nothing like so seasoned as Illingworth, who had 11 years' start, he has the kind of cricketing know-how an

Australian acquires in some 150 matches, including two tours of South Africa and once each through Britain and India. Much the same disparity has applied to other Aussie skippers touring England, yet with mostly younger captains the Australians have won five Tests to England's four over their last four visits.

Reports that London bookmakers are laying 6 to 4 on England don't worry a player aware that bookmakers are even less infallible than computers. 'We could hardly start favourites, seeing that England beat us last time and the 1972 series will be in English conditions,' he says. 'But the series against the World XI has given us a lift.'

Chappell has not been infected– and I hope he never will be– by the feverish neurosis that makes winning appear to be all that matters (even if shamelessly gained by gamesmanship) and makes defeat a disgrace. In realistic acceptance of the rough with the smooth, he shows signs that, with his ball sense, he has inherited sportsmanship, of which there's been no over-supply around lately.

In February Wally Langdon and other West Australians commended Chappell on the way his South Australians fielded in steady rain to enable a finish to be reached in Perth, though every few overs with a wet ball made it more likely that the drenched bowlers and fieldsmen would lose the match– and with it the Sheffield Shield. (As this was in a hot region, it would not do to take it as a precedent for Bradford!)

The Australians are playing better under Chappell, largely because they are showing more initiative and have regained some confidence. From the far edge of the generation gap, however, one critic of Ian's informality says his white towel hat is out of place in a Test match, without explaining why. Britain's climate – more temperate, shall we say? – should mostly spare Englishmen this affront to tradition.

*At The Oval in 1975 Ian Chappell announced his retirement from the captaincy of Australia after holding the post for a record 30 Tests. He marked the match, which was drawn, with a personal innings of 192. When his brother, Greg, took over the leadership against West Indies, Ian continued to make high scores in his own dashing manner, but his language and behaviour on the field forced the authorities to discipline him. He led Australia to 15 victories in seven series with ten drawn matches in four years which saw the Australian XI moulded into a tough and efficient fighting unit.—Ed.*

# PETER LEVER

## by John Arlott

*The Cricketer* July 1972

The heart of English cricket is the county game; and the essence of county cricket is not the Test star who dominates it but the ordinary county cricketer who is there every day and gives it his constant and fullest effort. He does not, like the representative players, miss a dozen county games a year to play for his country. He is the man for all seasons; county cricket is for him an achieved peak and a fulfilment. He is a recognisable, respected and relishable person; in his way a representative Englishman.

Once in a rare while, when opportunity and a peak spell of performance coincide, such a cricketer plays for England; and when that happens, the body of the game is splendidly happy for him.

Whatever may be argued about the Rest of the World series of 1970, it afforded passage into the England team for two of the most diligent craftsmen in the county game in Brian Luckhurst and Peter Lever. Brian Luckhurst was the least widely fancied of the three batsmen brought in to replace established men unavailable for the first match; but by the end of the rubber he had established his England place. Peter Lever had less room for manoeuvre. He replaced Greig in the last game of the series and, coming on as second change, after Snow, Old and Wilson, produced the best figures of his career – 7 for 83 – in the first innings of the World XI. They were the worthwhile wickets of Barlow, Graeme Pollock, Mushtaq, Sobers, Clive Lloyd, Procter and Intikhab. It was also his achievement that, when the Saturday crowd turned up to watch Pollock and Sobers continue their spectacular partnership of the previous day, they saw, instead, Peter Lever tying them down, putting them out and bowling himself into the side for Australia.

Peter Lever

Hardly any cricketer – least of all a pace bowler who has never taken a hundred wickets in a season – can hope to be chosen for England for the first time within a month of his thirtieth birthday and, when that happened to him, Peter Lever accepted it with the excitement and gratitude of a modest man. Since then he has rarely been out of the England side.

Omitted for the first Test in Australia, he bowled his way in for the second; proved an admirable foil to Snow in the decisive breakthrough in the fourth; was the most effective England bowler in the sixth; and, with three good and economical wickets in the first innings and Chappell's in the second, played an important part in the winning of the seventh which gave England the Ashes. It was soon obvious, too, that he was a good tourist.

Left out of the first Indian Test last summer, he came back in the second at Old Trafford when his 5 for 70 and an innings of 88 not out gave England the winning chance that was destroyed by rain. He has taken part in two valuable batting partnerships, both wicket records for those Test series: 149 – in 133 minutes – with Alan Knott for the seventh wicket against New Zealand, and 187 with Ray Illingworth for the eighth in the 1971 Indian Test at Lord's.

So he entered his benefit year on a far more exalted plane than he could have foreseen even two years ago. He belongs in the tradition of Lancashire professionals. Born in the 'border town' of Todmorden – since the 1890s legally in Yorkshire but Lancashire by virtue of being a cotton rather than a woollen town – he has the ancient gratitude for cricket as an alternative to the mill where he worked for six dragging months after leaving school. He first appeared for Lancashire in 1960 when he was 19; but he studied and served long and earnestly in the shadow of the England bowlers Brian Statham and Ken Higgs. He was not capped until 1965 and even in that season he played in only 14 of the county's 28 Championship matches. Subsequently the more explosive Ken Shuttleworth appeared superficially a better prospect, and was chosen in the first of the England-Rest of the World matches.

Peter Lever – as he cheerfully recognises – has come to his present standing through solid virtues rather than outstanding brilliance. He bowls at full effort: it may be argued that his run-up is too long but it is the approach of one set upon lifting his natural medium pace to the highest level consonant with control. His stamina – doggedly developed by regular cross-country running – and application are such that he can, and does, bowl long spells without loss of control or enthusiasm.

Finally, the spark which lifts him above some others is his ability to make the ball – new or worn – which pitches on the right-hander's stumps leave the bat late and with all the life the pitch will grant. These merits have made him an honest and respected performer on the highest level of cricket. He never expected so much – but he has earnt it – and he would not demand more.

His team-mates and his opponents like him for the basic virtues of integrity, modesty and diligence: and they do not miss his humour. To the spectator he is an engaging rather than an exciting figure with his wiry fair hair, pale, expressive face and angular, determined approach. He always bowls his best, trying, in the old manner, to get the batsman out with every ball.

Peter Lever belongs truly in, and to, the North Country; his travels make him the more appreciative of home, with his wife and three children, on the moorland edge of Rochdale. He took a three-year course at Leeds in physical education and has spent much time coaching young cricketers. Yet it is by no means certain that he will take that line after he leaves the county game. He has an alert mind, concerned with matters other then cricket, and he could yet make a mark outside the world of games.

*After an absence of two years, Peter Lever was recalled to England's Test team for the 1974–75 Australasian tour. In Australia he took none for 111 in the first Test, missed the middle four, and astounded the opposition with 6 for 38 on the first morning at Melbourne, placing Australia in a hopeless position. Then at Auckland, in the first New Zealand Test match, his name appeared on all the front pages when a short ball bowled by him to Ewen Chatfield, New Zealand's number eleven, knocked him unconscious. Chatfield's life was saved by immediate medical attention. Lever played once only against the 1975 Australians, taking his total of wickets to 41 (at 36.80) in 17 Tests spread across five years. —Ed.*

# BOB MASSIE

## by Richie Benaud

*The Cricketer* August 1972

The scoreboard at the WACA ground, Perth is a modern affair, a trifle dusty inside but certainly a cause for pride in the West where two years ago they successfully staged their first Test match.

Working in that board is more the task for an enthusias-tic youngster than a man setting himself to produce per-formances likely to gain a place in an Australian team to tour England. Robert Arnold Lockyer Massie did his scoreboard stint at the WACA on returning from a season in Scotland and his only regret from the Lord's Test may have been that the scoreboards in England – Nottingham excepted – never show the bowler's analysis.

His team-mates call him 'Fergie', a follow-up to the nicknaming style that is in vogue in Australian cricket these days. Massey-Ferguson are the tractor people and 'Fergie' is short for    well there you are! Bruce Francis is 'The Mule'; and Ashley Mallett is 'Rowdy' because before this tour he spoke very rarely and only when he had some-thing pertinent to say.

Massie overnight became the sensation of the cricket world when in the Lord's Test he swept aside the England batsmen as though they were wielding only the handles of the bats rather than an implement with blade attached.

No doubt the Australian medium-pacer will suffer his setbacks during this tour, but what a start he has made!

No-one can take away from him the statistical achieve-ments of having taken 16 wickets in his debut Test match ... and that at Lord's, so aptly described recently as the 'Cathedral of Cricket'. It is possible to take wickets by bowling badly, as I and many other bowlers can testify, but it is not possible to take eight in an innings doing so and then follow it up with another eight in the second innings.

111

Massie did this and he bowled superbly throughout, combining late movement in the air with splendid accuracy and the occasional movement off the pitch. I derived some amusement that day from the people who besieged – perhaps attacked is the better word – me with advice as to how the England batsmen should have countered Massie's bowling. Had that advice been conveyed to them and had they acted on it, we would have watched a wonderful spectacle: batsmen allowing the outswinger to pass and hitting the inswinger, or allowing the inswinger to pass and smashing the outswinger over cover point. In addition, they would have had to take block outside the leg stump, and on the leg, middle and off stumps; kept side-on in the stroke and opened their stance à la Barrington when the bowler operated around the wicket.

In the end they would have finished up like the bowler in that most magnificent of Rigby cartoons where he so perfectly depicted the problems associated with the front-foot law in cricket.

No . . . you could have thrown in any batsman from any country in any era on that Saturday at Lord's and they would have had the same problems with Massie.

There is a touch of irony in the fact that Massie started his cricketing life as a leg-spinner, giving the ball plenty of air to entice the batsmen down the pitch. All leg-spinners want to play Hamlet with the new ball at some stage of their careers; it just happens that Massie has done it very, very well.

Now he pins the batsmen like butterflies to the board, giving them little respite but always attacking them with his full length and his movement in the air. The ball is there to be driven if they wish to take the gamble, but the batsman's biggest problem is to have his feet in the right position for the drive, and not many can guarantee that at the moment. The swing is so late!

Alan Davidson is the last bowler to handle the new ball and make it move in the air so late that often the batsmen are committed to the stroke and have to compromise with the hurried, adjusting effort.

The big help of course has come from the new lbw Law

Bob Massie

that allows for the batsman to be given out even if not playing a stroke at the ball coming in from outside the off stump. No more of the pad thrusting at the ball swinging in – it has become something of a perilous venture. Add to that Massie's loose-flapping wrist and high action, and the opposing batsman certainly has plenty of problems.

There is no discernible change in body movement when Massie bowls his inswinger . . . or rather none that I can pick up, though rumour has it that the England batsmen feel they have been able to detect a difference between the body position of the two deliveries.

In its own way that could be very dangerous, for any batsman concentrating so hard on that may well be leaving himself open to other methods of attack, and sometimes even the bowler is surprised at a result in direct contrast with the one at which he has aimed.

Australian selectors are very astute people, and Massie and his partner Dennis Lillee were picked out as future Test prospects well before they ever stepped onto a Test arena. I had heard of Massie, vaguely, when I happened to see him bowl in a match in Australia and mentioned to Sir Donald Bradman the next time I saw him that I had been impressed. 'You're in good company then,' he said. Lillee was very raw when the Australian selectors picked *him* out as a future prospect and in the end they had to choose him before they really wanted to – against England in the Adelaide Test in 1971.

Now the West Australian pair are in harness in Test cricket and who would dare predict how long their partnership may last? Certainly they complement each other perfectly, Lillee with his blistering pace and sharp lift from short of a good length and Massie with his swing.

Looking in from outside I felt that Lillee took quite a few of Massie's wickets for him at Lord's by keeping up the pressure on the batsmen, and forcing them to try and score runs off the accurate bowling at the other end. Lillee now is fast, not quite as quick as Lindwall but one of these days he will be. It's no fun facing Lillee and knowing that at the other end the ball is moving around as though the bowler is pulling it on a string.

114

Massie's success would have been quite bearable for Australians, even if he had not been so likeable in himself. In fact, he is one of the quietest and most pleasant of men, enthusiastic on the field and a wonderful team man, ever eager to assist other players. Lillee is the same. In fact, to me, they are, off the field, the quietest 'pairing' of fast bowlers I have ever come across. Perhaps the best thing to underline that is to watch what happens the next time Massie takes a wicket in a Test match. There is all the enthusiasm and the backslapping and leaping about, but, as well, there is genuine pleasure from the other players at the success achieved by Massie. It couldn't, in fact, have happened to a nicer fellow.

*Such an auspicious Test debut was no preparation for the swiftness of Bob Massie's decline. He played three more times against England in that 1972 series, taking five wickets at Trent Bridge, none at Headingley, and two at The Oval. At home he took eight Pakistan wickets in two Tests, but a few weeks later, in West Indies, his form, after illness, was not strong enough to win a Test place. Nor has he played for Australia since or even held a regular place in the Western Australian side.—Ed.*

# KEITH STACKPOLE

## by Richie Benaud

*The Cricketer* September 1972

Old-time cartoons of cricketers generally depicted the flannelled fool as a slimly-built young man, clearly able to leap about in extraordinary fashion all over the park. As cricket-followers know, they come in all shapes and sizes these days, the Australians walking onto the field with the rangy Ashley Mallett alongside the squarely-built figure of Keith Stackpole.

Stackpole is more in the mould of the village blacksmith, or even your cheerful family butcher, though opposition bowlers get little pleasure ruminating over the fact that his well-fed appearance belies his quick footwork and fast reflexes.

At the time of writing, he leads the Australian batting averages for the Test series against England and he is averaging 15 runs an innings more than any other player in the home side. There are those in the England team who shake their heads when the ball flies over slip from an attempted square cut or runs off the edge from a straight drive. We all should give thanks that they have the privilege of cursing their ill luck . . . that so-called misfortune is the spectators' delight and I only wish there were more batsmen in the world willing to take their chance and hit the ball with the bat, rather than allow the opposite to take place.

Keith Raymond, he was christened back on July 10, 1940, at a time when his father, also Keith, was a top-line player in Victoria, where he played in the Sheffield Shield team. Keith senior was much like his son in the power of his cutting and hooking and both over the years have been a real strength to the Collingwood team in the hard-fought Melbourne first-grade competition.

Most cricketers know the younger Stackpole as 'Stacky'

Keith Stackpole

and that has been the case from the time he made his debut for Victoria at the age of 19. That game was first-class, but only against Tasmania, and it was three years before he gained a spot in the Sheffield Shield team.

From that point, it was only two years before he was playing for Australia against Mike Smith's MCC team of 1965–66, coming into the Adelaide Test and the last one played in Melbourne. He was then, as he is now, an attacking batsman with a genuine desire to add to the spectators' enjoyment of the game and a belief that the faster the batsmen score the more chance there is of winning the match.

At the same time, this early period of his cricket was marked by a real lack of experience in that far too often he was dismissed on the hook shot by bowlers deliberately 'feeding' him with the short-pitched delivery. Nowadays he is far more circumspect in that regard and, though he has been dismissed from the bouncer on the current tour, he has played the hook shot with discretion.

I suppose he is as close to being an ideal member of a touring team as it is possible to find, ever ready to practise, helpful with the younger players and, under that cheerful ruddy exterior, possessed of a fierce will to win. It was the high point of his career to be named vice-captain for this tour of England and he and Ian Chappell have worked well together on all aspects of the cricket over the past few months. Stackpole's has been a gradual elevation to the top in Australian cricket, and he has had some hard times as well as successes. At one point his batting form was such that his place in the national team must have been in some jeopardy and it wasn't really until he began to open with Lawry that his form entitled him automatically to a place in the side.

Against West Indies in Australia, in 1968–69, he had a good series and some fine performances in the Shield matches, and then against India and South Africa, on that ill-fated tour, he again scored over 1000 runs. Around this time he was batting with tremendous confidence, hooking and cutting and extending his range with many more front-foot strokes.

When England came to Australia under Ray Illingworth's leadership it was Stackpole who carried the attack to the faster bowlers right from the first Test played in Brisbane.

Then he hit a brilliant 207, with the bowlers becoming more and more frustrated and more and more convinced that in the end the ebullient right-hander must get an edge to slip or be caught on the hook.

It was an expensive lesson and one they heeded with their bowling tactics for the rest of the series. Stackpole made over 600 runs in the six Tests played on that tour and, when he batted just as well in the series against the Rest of the World, he was one of the first men chosen for England.

There was a time when his slow bowling earned him the courtesy title of all-rounder . . . but now he bowls rarely in Test or Sheffield Shield matches. Probably the reason for this is his elevation to the top of the batting order and a consequent desire to concentrate fully on the job in hand, rather than take the chance of being tired late in the day if he has to bat for the last half hour. As a change bowler he is quite useful though he doesn't spin the ball very much . . . most of the time it hurries off the pitch more like a top-spinner than a leg-break. In some ways it is probably a good thing he has forsaken the ball for the bat, for Australia had at one stage developed a dangerous tendency to class as an all-rounder anyone who could bat well and be used as a change bowler. Far better the situation now, where Lillee, Massie, and one spinner form the backbone of the attack and allow the batsmen to get on with their task of hitting the ball to provide a target at which the bowlers can bowl.

Stackpole's batting method is, to me, beautifully simple. If the ball is a half volley . . . hit it for four! If it is short . . . hook or cut for four!

If you can't get four then take three or two or a quick single and, if that is impossible, then play it defensively. Add to that the fact that he doesn't much mind if it is the first ball of the innings or the last and it is easy to see why he is an extremely popular player with spectators in all cricket countries where he has toured.

Before this year his only experience of English pitches was one season in the Lancashire League.

There was a school of thought that he might have difficulty with his method of concentrating on the back-foot strokes but, like any really good batsman, Stackpole adjusted his batting to the conditions.

At 32, he is one of the oldest players in the team but still has plenty of cricket left in him for Australia and for Victoria. The pleasant thing to contemplate is that whenever and wherever he plays it will always be worth the price of admission to watch him bat. There are some players for whom it would be difficult to journey across the road . . . for Stackpole and his powerful right hand it is worth going many a mile.

*Keith Stackpole retired from first-class cricket after Australia's tour of New Zealand in 1974, finishing his career with 2807 runs in 43 Tests, average 37.42, with seven centuries. In his final Test, at Auckland, he 'bagged a pair'. His lusty approach was missed at the start of Australia's innings but was responsible for some trenchant comment under his name in a book of reminiscence and in newspaper columns.—Ed.*

# FAROKH ENGINEER

## by Mike Stevenson

*The Cricketer* October 1972

First slip in the Lancashire side is known as Butlin's. Catches come and occasionally go but with astonishing regularity a flurry of pads, gloves and Engineer will intervene followed by a predatory shriek and another batsman is on his way to the pavilion.

Basically there are two varieties of 'keeper, the unobtrusive and the flamboyant, and it is because one is presuming a small percentage of readers who are not conversant with his style of play that I point out the fact that Engineer belongs to the latter category. I wonder how he would have turned out if he had been coached (but this question is purely academic)?

Engineer, like Alan Knott and Godfrey Evans, is an entertainer. Something in his psychological make-up precludes his being able to achieve a position where he is waiting calmly for the arrival of the ball like a Tallon, an Andrew or a Grout.

Mention of the last-named reminds me of a recent conversation with Neil Hawke, as talented a bowler as he is entertaining as a raconteur: 'If you threw in the ball to Wally Grout just a bit off target,' he said, 'you'd get the full treatment. One hell of a glare and something like: "These hands are my life. Protect them".'

I asked him about Farokh Engineer: 'He's the most Australian Indian I've ever met. He was one of us.' It was this admirable ability to fit in, to identify himself with the fortunes of his new environment that made his arrival at Old Trafford in 1968 such a happy event.

Engineer first played cricket at the surprisingly mature age of 17 at Don Bosco High School, Bombay, having captained his school at both hockey and football, but his introduction to the game at a high standard came when he went to Bombay University, which he represented from the outset, getting his first taste of representative cricket when selected for Combined Universities *v* West Indies in 1958–59, his debut in Test cricket following in 1961–62.

After a period of disfavour he was recalled to the Indian Test side in '66 and had the distinction of scoring 94 not out before lunch against the front-line West Indies bowlers. 'I had no idea,' he told me, 'that another six runs would have put me in the record books in very distinguished company, but I didn't get the strike much just before lunch and the chance slipped by.'

His philosophy which underlies his attitude to the game is that it is crucially important to give and to get enjoyment from playing. He is as uninhibited in his wicketkeeping as a performing seal and in the last Gillette Cup final, which Lancashire won to register their third successive triumph in this competition, he was accused by one writer (who should know better) of dropping seven catches. 'I couldn't believe my eyes when I read it. Thick edges out of my reach and leg byes, they were all chances to that man sitting up there in the Press box,' he said to me as much amused as irritated. 'Of course if you don't go for them but just watch them to the boundary then they're not chances. Honestly, I was really proud to stop some of those so-called "chances".'

So far I have said relatively little of his batting which, considering the massive talent of his 'keeping, might be regarded by some almost as a bonus. I described one of his more explosive innings not so long ago as being compounded of an inspired mixture of golf, squash and hockey. He was most affronted and took me severely to task. 'Every shot I played was orthodox,' he said. Frankly it didn't look like that to me and I'm sure it didn't to the bowlers.

It is true that his defence on the relatively rare occasions that one has seen it employed for any length of time is orthodox but when he moves in to the drive the left elbow is glued into the left side so that the power of the shot whips the ball from off stump, and outside even, wide of mid-on in a manner that may offend the purist but extends the scorers.

Farokh Engineer

He is a great improviser but never loath to 'charge' a bowler. His hooking and 'flat-bat' cover-driving are formidable and reflect the quick eye, the natural talent of his wicketkeeping and the fact (that one should never forget in assessing his play) that he is entirely uncoached.

It would be stupid to underestimate his ability as a batsman. He reminds me of the old story of George Hirst, pulling away merrily at Lord's when one Old Etonian elegant turned to the other and said, 'Oh, my god! Just look at that stroke', whereupon an emigrant from the Bradford area, unable to maintain silence, turned upon them and replied: 'Aye. And look at t'bloody scoreboard.'

However much Engineer is at home in England, he has never cut or wanted to cut home ties and was thrilled at his selection in the last India/England series. He is a happy person and one who is outstandingly pleasant with children, remembering perhaps the friendliness and kindness of 'Polly' Umrigar, when he, Farokh, was a young lad.

He is a lively and amusing companion.

Some time ago Peter Lever had bowled superbly well at Lord's to win a hard-fought match for Lancashire. Sir Neville Cardus came into the Lancashire dressing room to congratulate him. 'I'm sure,' said Sir Neville, 'that you must be proud today to be a Lancastrian.'

'Nay,' said Lever, 'I was born in Todmorden. That's in Yorkshire, Sir Neville.' And a voice from behind them, that of Farokh Engineer, muttered darkly: 'Bloody foreigner!'

*One of Test cricket's senior players, Farokh Engineer is still keeping wicket efficiently and playing the occasional innings of note. In the fifth Test of the 1972–73 series against England, opening the innings, he hit 121 at Bombay. He remains a popular and important member of the Lancashire XI, who added yet another Gillette Cup triumph to their list of recent honours in 1975.—Ed.*

# B. S. CHANDRASEKHAR

## by K. N. Prabhu

*The Cricketer* January 1973

Cricket, it is said, is a game of glorious uncertainties. The phrase could well apply to the careers of certain players. Like many illustrious players of the past, Bhagwat Subramaniam Chandrasekhar, India's trump bowler in the series of 1971 against England, has had his share of ups and downs. His performance earned him a place in *Wisden*. Yet only the season before he was in the wilderness.

His very future was in doubt. The Australians – it seemed a deliberate tactic – had hit him out of the attack in the series of 1967–68 and, due to an ankle injury, he was summarily sent home after the second Test.

He attempted to stage a comeback against Bill Lawry's Australians in the season of 1969–70; he was rejected, for he failed to give Prasanna the support he needed which might have enabled South Zone to beat the Australians on a dusty Bangalore wicket. After his failure in the pre-trial matches for the West Indies he was practically written off as one of India's attacking bowlers.

But while India were in West Indies he won the attention of the selectors by his sustained performances in the Ranji Trophy. Even then his selection was thought to be a bit of a 'gamble'. How that gamble paid off is now history.

Chandrasekhar, born on May 18, 1945, grew to accept the rough with the smooth. When he was five years old he was struck down by polio. It left him with a withered arm. It may have embittered others, but it gave Chandra the courage and confidence that enabled him to face the 'mutabilities of fortune' in later years. He accepted his disability with typical fortitude and put it to good use. Indeed, it can be said that he turned the handicap into

125

an asset. His withered right arm could be coiled and unleashed like a spring to provide a fizzer of a top-spinner. There have been occasions when it has been quick enough to bowl what could be taken for a bouncer.

Unlike most Indian Test players, Chandra did not 'graduate' to big cricket through schools and university competitions. He was just past his seventeenth birthday when he was picked on the basis of his performance for his club to play for Mysore in the Ranji Trophy. With 25 wickets in four Ranji Trophy matches he won his place in the South Zone team for the Duleep Trophy. A couple of months later, he had arrived in Test cricket.

We first heard of him during the Duleep Trophy of 1963. West Zone, with their strong concentration of batsmen, were puzzled by a bowler with a long orthodox name and an unorthodox action, who bowled top-spinners and googlies, with an occasional leg-break at medium pace. We had become accustomed to the leisurely action of Gupte, the stereotyped and stilted run-up and rolled leg-breaks of Borde. Chandra's bowling was a new phenomenon.

And that was what it seemed to MCC on the tour of 1963–64, when they came up against him in the Bombay Test, in which he bagged 4 for 67. The drugged wickets, on which the ball double-declutched – as Cowdrey pointed out in an issue of *The Cricketer* – did not allow him much scope. He took 10 wickets at 33.90 from 161.3 overs.

There were, however, some who felt that he was in danger of being used as a stock bowler. But Chandra's reputation was firmly established the following year, when the Australians played a three-Test series on their way home from England. He bowled India to victory at Bombay with figures of 4 for 50 and 4 for 73. These were to be bettered at The Oval in 1971. I can still see in my mind's eye the ball that decided the Bombay Test. It pitched on the leg stump and whipped across to hit the top of the off stump. Burge, who had made top score of 80 in the first innings, lifted his bat and tapped the blade in tribute. A similar master ball accounted for Edrich at The Oval to swing the match in India's favour.

After his bowling against Simpson's men, there was no

B. S. Chandrasekhar

denying Chandra's place in an Indian team. He had the West Indies on the run in the Bombay Test of 1966–67, but poor catching cost India a game that should have been closer than the scores indicated. He finished with 18 wickets at 28.5 apiece in that rubber from 196.5 overs, twice as many as that sent down by any other bowler.

There was a danger of his being used as a hack. And this was evident when he finished with 57 wickets, including 16 in the Tests, from about 700 overs in the England tour of 1967. He won notice, but could have been more effective had his bowling received the support it did in the field in the glorious summer of 1971.

Chandra was worked to death on the East African 'safari' which was tagged on to the tour of England. And there were barely two months before he was chosen for the ill-starred tour of Australia. He was tipped to succeed on the fast Australian wickets. But he had gone stale, losing in line, length and direction. He was sent home in mid-tour – back to his job as a junior bank executive.

A lesser man may have expressed his resentment at this scurvy treatment. But Chandrasekhar never once referred to it, for his injury could have healed with attention. But off-spin was a more potent weapon against the Australians, the batting had to be reinforced by flying out Jaisimha, and the most easily dispensable player was the meekest of them all, Chandrasekhar. After what happened in the summer of 1971, as he ran amok at The Oval, his shirt-tails flapping, it seemed only just that the meek should inherit the earth.

*The 1972–73 series against England found Chandrasekhar in marvellous form: he took a record 35 wickets in five Tests at 18.91, including 8 for 79 at Delhi in the first of the series. Vagaries of form, always most noticeable with this precious species of bowler, have precluded him from regular selection, and a finger injury in the Lord's Test of 1974 set him back. Fourteen West Indies wickets in 1974–75 cost him 41 apiece, and it remained clear that here was an 'original', but one who needed to be used as an instrument of attack and not as a stock bowler.—Ed.*

# GREG CHAPPELL

## by David Frith

*The Cricketer* February 1973

When, in March 1970, Lawry's Australians sorrowfully disembarked after their disastrous tour of South Africa, Australian cricket was just about out on its feet. Perhaps the biggest disappointment – if the invoice of 333 runs for McKenzie's sole Test wicket be overlooked – was Ian Chappell, who had been flagrantly billed by his captain at the start of the series as 'the world's best batsman'. The Springboks shattered that daring claim in a whirl of bouncers and yorkers, and signalised with a bewildering four-nil victory what can now be seen as their last contest before banishment from international cricket.

Australia was stunned. The end was nigh.

But the worriers should have known better. History's pattern is there, like an alluvial meadow, producing crops from hidden seeds after even the hardest winter.

Although Australia next opposed England – and lost – the beginnings of a revival were soon apparent. Chappell's younger brother, Greg, was brought into the side for the second Test of the 1970–71 series, and he was prompt in writing his name into the record books and inside his green cap – in indelible ink.

He walked to the crease at Perth when Australia were 107 for 5 in reply to England's 397. In four and a half hours he scored 108, and with Redpath, who made a stoic 171, Chappell added 219. He fought very hard for his half-century, but in the evening as shadows lengthened and the bowlers' feet ached he plundered his last fifty in an hour.

He was 22 years of age and the toast of his country.

He had entered first-class cricket at 18 and registered his first century that same season (1966–67), a gritty innings played in Brisbane's cloying heat and humidity and with the painful after-effects of a poisoned foot. With a college-boy freshness but uncompromising mien he had passed through the extra-mural examination of county cricket with Somerset, developing month by month, making the first Sunday League century, bowling at medium pace well enough on one occasion to take 7 for 40 against Yorkshire (having earlier been a leg-spinner), and broadening both his experience on wet wickets and his philosophy with a 'pair' at the hands of Geoff Arnold (balanced within months by two centuries in a match for South Australia against Queensland).

His most satisfying innings was a century on a slow turner at Weston-super-Mare against Middlesex.

He failed in his second Test match (the Sydney débâcle), missed out again at Melbourne, and fell to Lever without scoring at Adelaide Oval, the home ground of his grandfather, Vic Richardson, and now, with younger brother Trevor having joined Ian and Greg (all products of Prince Alfred College) in the South Australia side, 'the Chappells' own paddock'.

Then came the decider, the seventh Test, at Sydney. And after Greg's three-hour 65 had helped Australia to a first-innings lead of 80 they needed, with five wickets in hand, 100 runs for a victory which would have levelled the series and saved the Ashes.

That fifth day opened with Greg Chappell and Rod Marsh in possession. One can only say in support of their increased stature today that had it been the 1973 models Chappell and Marsh the result would have been a foregone conclusion and Australia should have been safe. As it was, Marsh fell through inexperience and an Illingworth kicker left Chappell stranded. England finished two-up and Australia were left wistful and with vengeful eye.

Those in opposition who saw Greg Chappell as a growing threat in future years searched for weaknesses and concluded that he was too on-sided. But he was a growing man, a Test centurion, the most exciting prospect his country had had since Walters. The leg-sidedness would doubtless take care of itself.

And it did. By 1972 he was an all-round batsman, playing positively through the covers, through mid-off, and, to the relief of those who earlier had enjoyed his on-side play, the

130

Greg Chappell

original crack off the toes was there in all its glory. He was a charm to watch: confident and unruffled, a lesson to all from within his cocoon of concentration. Until he was dismissed Australia always stood a chance. When he *was* out England relaxed just a shade.

Tall, with an upright almost Edwardian stance, he makes, when he drives, a characteristically strong commitment to the front foot; the body bends forward over the fulcrum of the braced left leg, giving him such a commanding airborne view of the oncoming ball that it is the plainest formality that it should be dispatched with power and certain placing all along the ground. And the manner in which the right foot kicks high behind the stroke is nothing less than arrogant.

There is little in his style to suggest his teenage inspirations, Neil Harvey and Bob Simpson.

Somerset did try to entice him back at a salary higher than any previously offered but Chappell declined, believing that so much continuous cricket could be detrimental in the long term.

During the season which separated the two Anglo-Australian rubbers Australia took on 'the Rest of the World', and for the home side's batting the two Chappells with Stackpole bestrode the series – after Greg had sat out the first two matches as twelfth man. He re-entered international competition with 115 not out at Melbourne, 197 not out at Sydney, and 85 at Adelaide, and sudden doubts about his inclusion for the tour of England were forgotten.

In 1972 Chappell, with the bat, and Lillee, with the ball (with Chappell either crouching menacingly at short leg or grasping everything within reach at third slip), were, with Stackpole's valiant consistency at Number 1, Marsh's redoubtable form, and Massie's surrealist performance at Lord's, the main forces in Australia's implicit dominance of an ideal Test series.

Greg, having made a technically admirable 131 at Lord's – the innings of the series – came near to earning the freedom of London by scoring another hundred at The Oval in the fifth Test. This time brother Ian also reached three figures as coolly and undemonstratively they constructed a stand of 201 for the second wicket.

Incredibly it was only the second time they had added a hundred in tandem, but it revived thoughts of the Woodfull-McCabe, Bradman-Ponsford, Barnes-Morris brand of batting dependability.

The match was won, the series squared, and the team went home; but not before the captain had paid public though subtle tribute to his brother's standing. He suggested that he himself would never be the accomplished batsman that Greg now was, but he was careful not to damn him with claims too lavish. He remembered how that could rebound.

Some months later the brothers were making masterful Test centuries against Pakistan. Such is the new dynasty.

Gregory Stephen Chappell, it may be reflected, came into the world just a week before Bradman's scoreless final Test, in 1948, which nevertheless was a good year for Australian cricket. Now there are some who would say it was a wonderful year for Australian cricket.

*Greg Chappell was appointed captain of Australia for the series against West Indies which began at Brisbane in November 1975. He scored 123 in the first innings and 109 not out in the second, and his side won by eight wickets. Only weeks before, everyone had been asking how one of the world's premier batsmen could go through seven innings in a series against England for only one success (73 not out) and another 33 paltry runs. Previously his skill at the crease had passed almost every examination: 247 not out and 133 against New Zealand at Wellington, two centuries against England a year later. All that remained was for his tactical abilities to be tested at international level; his leadership of Queensland, where he transferred in 1973–74, indicated that he was the man for the job and in leading Australia to a five-one victory over West Indies he contributed 702 runs from his own bat (average 117). Not only one of the finest batsmen in the game, Greg Chappell was now captain of probably the best team in the world.—Ed.*

# TONY GREIG

## by Alan Gibson

*The Cricketer* March 1973

In an era of tall men, it is still his height that strikes you, on the twentieth time of watching as much as the first. Find a dozen skeletons so long on a Pacific island, and you would declare you had found a race of giants. He is six feet seven and a half inches tall. Naturally, his height conditions his cricket, just as it conditions Pilling's cricket. I doubt if a cricketer has any real advantage over others in being either tall or short (compare Woolley and Hendren) but it makes a difference to his style, and also to what spectators expect of him. Thus when Greig goes right down the pitch and gets hold of a drive, or when he leaps high in the air, or dives yards away to hold a catch, we say, 'That's the advantage of being tall'; but when he is late on a yorker, or cannot hold a slip catch straight at his ankles (I am not suggesting he does either of these things often), 'Ah!' we say wiseacrely, 'that's the trouble with these tall men.' I heard this said once at Hove last season so severely that you would have thought the man ought to be doing something about it, perhaps going on a diet to lose a few inches of height.

A. W. Greig is 26. He was born in Queenstown, South Africa, and as his name suggests came from a Scottish family. He played first-class cricket for Border in the 1965–66 season, and in 1966 made his first appearance for Sussex. His general physique had not then quite grown to match his height; he looked like a cherub on stilts; but quickly the word went round that here was a fine player. He played for the county against Cambridge (he was still qualifying), scoring 51 for once out and taking three wickets. For the second eleven he scored 362 runs and took 42 wickets. In 1967, he was in the side for the first Championship match against Lancashire at Hove, and scored 156 not out in less than four hours. Statham, Higgs and Lever were bowling.

Tony Greig

Later that season, also at Hove, he took 8 for 25 in Gloucestershire's second innings, winning the match. He scored 1299 runs and took 67 wickets that season. His form was still in-and-out, and was to remain so for some time, but he had arrived.

In 1968 he did not do quite so well, but was still a redeeming part of a Sussex side for which everything went wrong (they were bottom of the Championship). In 1969 he again scored 1000 runs, and took 69 wickets. Sussex did better but were still in the process of sorting themselves out, and so I suppose was Greig, who had to consider his cricketing future in difficult circumstances. He decided that he would play Test cricket, if chosen, for England. I have no idea of what his motives were, but however you look at it, it must have been a courageous decision.

He was justified, so far as his cricket went, in the short term; and he has been abundantly vindicated in his belief in himself in the long term; but he must have had a few worried moments in between. In 1970 he was chosen for three of the matches against the Rest of the World. In the second match at Nottingham, which England won (probably the best performance by an England side since the Second World War) he had as much as anyone to do with victory, taking four wickets in the first innings and three in the second. The batsmen whose wickets he took were Richards (twice), Sobers (twice), Kanhai, Engineer and Barlow.

In the third match he took no wickets, but scored 55 and 22. He took 4 for 86 in the first innings of the Rest of the World in the fourth match at Leeds, but he did not bowl well in that innings. Indeed, he lost himself his place in the side, and we could see him doing it while he was bowling. When the Rest of the World batted on the morning of the second day both the pitch and the atmosphere favoured fast-medium seam bowlers, but Greig, though he produced a good ball from time to time, could not find a steady length or line. I remember how Trevor Bailey was itching with irritation that he could not be bowling himself.

Greig would no doubt have kept himself in the selectors' picture with some runs, but scored 5 and 0. So he was out of the last match and not chosen for Australia. He still scored 1000 runs in the season, and took 59 wickets, but his bowling average was higher than his batting. Yet he looked every long inch a cricketer, and his reputation as a close fielder (31 catches that year) was growing fast. If he was inconsistent, he was still young.

Perhaps he will look back on 1971 as the decisive season in his career. He again averaged fewer with the bat than the ball, but he scored a thousand runs and took 77 wickets; more importantly, bowling almost 800 overs to get them. Snow was flitting into and out of the Sussex side this season, and Greig had to carry the burden, both shock and stock as they used to say. The way in which he sustained his task put to rest any lingering doubts about his physical strength.

Hutton was preferred to him in the England side, but there was a general feeling that they were of much the same level, and that Greig would be the better when he could get the best out of himself. Both went to Australia that winter with the Rest of the World side. No doubt both were chosen in the first place because of Australian determination not to pick a Rest of the World side that approximated to the real strength of the Rest of the World: but it did not turn out to be so pointless a series as was intended, and of the two English all-rounders it was Greig who made his mark. It was now we began to hear of those astonishing catches close to the wicket, his long shadow stretching across the pitch.

Thus to the series against Australia last summer, and against India and Pakistan this winter. As I write, after the second Test against India, he seems to be the outstanding member of the side, and I notice that the cricket correspondent of *The Times*, the Sage of Longparish, has spoken especially highly of him. (The Sage of Longparish is not himself a tall man, and has not always been enthusiastic about Greig in the past. What he really feels is that all the best cricketers are five feet three. A judgment from this quarter is therefore convincing.)

I have not myself seen enough of Greig's cricket to offer a judgment; except to say that whatever he is doing on the field he is enjoyable to watch, and not just because that height catches the eye, nor that blond hair is so readily identifiable to a struggling commentator. He is a true athlete now; and still with a touch of the cherub.

*The captaincy of England came Tony Greig's way after the Edgbaston débâcle against Australia in 1975, and for the remaining three Tests of the series there was a marked revival in spirit and approach. His development had been steady and his emergence as a 'personality' dramatic and not always according to Hoyle. India loved him, especially when he picked up little Viswanath and cradled him when he reached his century; West Indies were uncertain of him when he ran out Kallicharran as the final ball of the day was played; Australia loved him and hated him as he mocked their bowlers while batting. He has scored Test hundreds fairly frequently and wavered between fast-medium and off-break bowling, taking 13 wickets in a Port-of-Spain Test on one celebrated occasion. As an intimidator of batsmen he has scourged all opposition. His colourful performances have made him valuable commercially and much sought after.—Ed.*

# MIKE PROCTER

## by Alan Gibson

*The Cricketer* June 1973

I suppose that most cricketers would say that now M. J. Procter is the best all-rounder in the world, and I agree, so far as such vague and unprovable tributes can be said to mean anything. He *is* a marvellous cricketer, beyond denial, though his bowling action has caused a scratching of heads among the orthodox. Not that there has ever been any suggestion of unfairness, of throwing: it is just that the strain he imposes upon himself every time he bowls a really fast ball, or even a moderately fast ball, seems more than a human frame can possibly withstand for long.

When Procter joined the Gloucestershire side in 1968, David Green (also a recent arrival) said after the pre-season practices: 'This bloke bowls at a hundred miles an hour from extra cover off the wrong foot.'

'Off the wrong foot': it is a phrase with a long cricket history, but nobody had examined what it meant, nor indeed could, until slow-motion film enabled us to see how bowlers actually delivered the ball. Racehorses, as you will see from old pictures, were usually drawn, when galloping, with all four legs stretched out at the same time. Slow-motion film of Procter shows that at the moment of delivery it is his left, or orthodox, foot which is in contact with the ground. But I dare say this would have been true of all the supposed 'wrong-foot' bowlers of the past. Certainly Procter is a wrong-footed bowler, as the term has customarily been used. Even on a soft pitch, he does not dig a pit. His pace comes from the last-second circular whip of his arm, his power is generated by his very strong shoulders. His long run is a stimulus to him, and an alarming sight for the batsmen. He does not believe he can bowl really fast without it. Much of cricket is played in the mind.

As for bowling 'from extra-cover', he often uses every

139

inch of the bowling crease. To vary the angle of delivery has always been a good quality of a bowler, and in fact Procter not only bowls from extra-cover but, when he feels like it, from mid-on. When he switches to bowling 'round the wicket', batsmen are inclined to suspect a deep plot or some sudden treachery in the pitch, but I expect he usually does it because he likes a change, just as he varies the length of his run-up with no logic, except the logic of how he feels (the best of arguments, given only that you are a good enough bowler: *cf* K. R. Miller).

Procter first came to England in 1965, along with Richards; two unknown South African youngsters wondering whether to go into the English county game. They played for Gloucestershire 2nd XI while qualifying for the county. I remember seeing them as spectators, watching a Somerset match at the Imperial Ground, Bristol: two slight, shy boys they seemed then, baffled by their surroundings. Their figures for Gloucestershire 2nd XI that season were:

| Batting | Ins | NO | R | HS | Av. |
|---|---|---|---|---|---|
| M. J. Procter | 24 | 7 | 527 | 80 | 31.00 |
| B. A. Richards | 26 | 5 | 632 | 81* | 30.09 |

| Bowling | O | M | R | W | Av. |
|---|---|---|---|---|---|
| B. A. Richards | 158 | 46 | 392 | 29 | 13.51 |
| M. J. Procter | 393 | 114 | 731 | 53 | 13.79 |

Between them in the batting averages came D. Bevan, and closely after them in the bowling averages came M. Ashenden, and I do not remember anyone saying *at the time* that Procter and Richards were noticeably better prospects than Bevan and Ashenden.

At the end of the season, Procter and Richards decided to go home. It was the 'instant qualification' clause that later decided them to return to England (Richards to Hampshire), and though it is true that the increase of overseas players has deprived many young English cricketers of chances, it is also worth remembering what an amount of pleasure these two have given since they appeared regularly in English summers.

Mike Procter

Procter's development as a cricketer has been much influenced by Gloucestershire, because Gloucestershire in his time have needed a hundred wickets from him more than two thousand runs. In South Africa, where he scored his six successive centuries in 1970–71 (equalling the record of Fry and Bradman, though possibly in less taxing circumstances), he has been able to do more justice to his batting. Even so, I have always felt that Gloucestershire put him in too high in the order. He has great strength, but he is mortal, and nobody can be expected to take all the wickets and score all the runs on seven days of a week. Of course, it is always tempting to put him in early, because he can win a match in an hour, and he is always prepared to try. But that bowling action must take a lot out of the strongest man, and he has suffered a good many strains and breaks in the last year or two.

Two of his innings recur to me: the more recent the one he played against Somerset in the Benson & Hedges competition in 1972. I forget how many he made, well over a hundred, and I remember that he was dropped when 40 or so, but he demolished Somerset, and the variety and power of his strokes in the latter part of that innings I have never seen equalled (think again? No, I have never seen them equalled, even if it *was* a one-day bun-fight).

The other innings was quite different. In the fourth match between England and the Rest of the World in 1970, the Rest needed 223 to win in the last innings, and were 75 for 5 overnight, with Richards and Kanhai unfit (though both did bat on the last day). Procter came in to join Richards with eight wickets down, and 40 still wanted. From the way he played the first ball, plumb in the middle, it was clear he intended to win the match, and so he did. He scored 22 not out, and it does not sound much, but there was an authority about the innings which forbade any suggestion that he would ever get out.

There are, on the other hand, times when he seems to take his cricket casually. The appearance can be deceptive, and anyway a man who does so much work is entitled to an occasional breather. He is inclined, perhaps, to present to the world a picture of himself as one of the flannelled fools.

But he has a generous and flexible mind, and his reactions to the problems at present facing South African cricketers have been honest, brave and even liberal.

*Mike Procter's seventh Test appearance for South Africa against Australia was destined to be his last. He became an all-year-round cricketer for Rhodesia and Gloucestershire. The grind of county cricket tended to take the edge off his speed, and eventually a knee injury compelled him to resort to off-breaks. An attempted comeback as a fast bowler in the Gillette Cup semi-final at Old Trafford in 1975 ended tragically when the knee, upon which he had had a ligament transplant, gave way.—Ed.*

# KEITH FLETCHER

## by Gordon Ross

*The Cricketer* July 1973

Of the England players in India, Keith Fletcher played the Indian triumvirate of world-class spinners with greater confidence than anyone else. To his colleagues in county cricket this came as no real surprise; he has always been a good player against spin, and it is this facet of cricket which gives him the most enjoyment. He feels that it is a genuine contest of skill being pitted against skill, with all the virtues of the game at stake, whereas batting against the less talented seam bowler, whose principal aim is to keep runs down, is a test of patience and temperament; both have their place in cricket, especially in Test cricket, but patience and temperament are not so much the ingredients for the spectator.

Of these Indian masters of spin, Fletcher rates Chandra as the most difficult proposition for the first half an hour of an innings; his pace and bounce combined need infinite pains when you are finding your bearings, but overall he regards Bedi as the best spinner in the world. Playing Bedi is a great challenge.

Fletcher, at 29, has a wealth of cricketing experience to his credit, beginning when he first played for the Cambridgeshire village of Caldecote, at the tender age of eleven.

He did not play for his school because the school was not large enough to support a cricket team, but it did have a net and a concrete wicket; this was the hatchery from which young Fletcher emerged, and was recommended to Essex at the age of thirteen.

At the same age he joined Royston to get club cricket experience. For Essex Young Amateurs and for Royston he had his first taste of good wickets and began to learn what the game is all about.

Keith Fletcher

Today he is a shrewd tactician and can probably analyse the faults in a cricketer's technique quicker than anyone; he has a great sense of the game which enables him to read a situation at first glance, an asset of which the Essex captain has been pleased to avail himself in the day-to-day sphere of activities.

Fletcher's true ability has never been accurately reflected in his performances for England, until, perhaps, the recent tour. Now he stands on the fringe of selection for six Test matches this summer.

For such a good player – an excellent driver – his disappointing results in Tests have baffled the connoisseurs, and a number of reasons, not least of which was temperament, were put forward. Truthfully, it is probably a variety of reasons, not so much temperament as adjustment to the atmosphere of a Test match, adjustment to having one good bowler follow another in Test cricket, and most of all, perhaps, the breaks. Luck consistently deserts the man who needs it most. When his luck turns, confidence is restored, and runs are so much easier to get.

In the environment of one of the happiest parties to tour overseas, Fletcher seems to have found what he was looking for, and the results should follow. This was a tour, he says, of enormous team spirit. Often when you went out to bat the batsman already at the crease would walk down the wicket and say, 'Shall I take Chandra for an over or two, until you get the feel of the wicket?' This was something he had never experienced in Test cricket before.

He came into the Essex side in 1962, for the first time, against Glamorgan at Ebbw Vale, under the captaincy of Trevor Bailey. It was against Glamorgan that he played his finest innings to date, in the summer of 1972. Essex, facing a Glamorgan total of 338 for 9 declared, were looking for bonus points. They declared at 350 for one, after Fletcher and Saville had added 288 in two hours and fifty minutes. Fletcher hit four sixes and 24 fours; not only did Essex finish the match with 22 points – they won it.

Fletcher's score of 181 not out was still not his highest; he hit 228 not out against Sussex at Hastings in 1968, the year in which he played his first Test match; so began a

146

Test career of trials and tribulations. Now, one hopes, in this, his benefit summer, his talents will flow as they should at the highest level.

As his fielding shows, he has the quickest of eyes and reflexes, and an abiding passion for sport. He hunts, shoots, used to play hockey and football – in fact anything knocking a ball about, and he does it well.

Like many batsmen before him, he always enjoys talking about his bowling and the 4 for 50 that he took for the MCC Under-25 team at Peshawar in the winter of 1966–67, when his leg-spinning reached its peak!

He talks of bowlers with greater enthusiasm than batsmen, of the enormous regard he has for Tom Cartwright– a magnificent artiste and a true professional. He tells of the fastest piece of bowling he ever faced– Fred Trueman on a rock-hard green-top, faster than Wes Hall in Kingston, Jamaica; his ambition is for Essex to win the Gillette Cup this season, so that their marvellous supporters can have one great day to remember, and that the players can play for Essex before a full house at Lord's.

No-one has better epitomised the character of the man than Fletcher's current Essex captain, Brian Taylor, when he said of him. 'He's the most unselfish player in the game. We all want him to do well.'

Those sentiments will be echoed far beyond the boundaries of Essex.

*Perhaps the major casualty of England's unhappy series in Australia in 1974–75 was Keith Fletcher, whose attempts to play fast bowlers Lillee and Thomson bordered on the pathetic. He gathered himself together sufficiently to make his highest Test score (216) against New Zealand at the end of the Australian tour, but when confronted by the Australians again in England his technique proved once more to be inadequate. Yet he remains one of the most attractive batsmen in the world when moving freely and attacking the bowling. Now captain of Essex, it is an inconceivable thought that he will not continue to play a large part in English cricket.—Ed.*

# BEVAN CONGDON

## by R. T. Brittenden

*The Cricketer* August 1973

There have been no more telling tributes to the works of
C. S. Forester: Bevan Congdon was reading a Hornblower
tale as New Zealand fought its memorable Trent Bridge
battle against England.

It may seem strange that a Test captain could read a book
as his team, on the fifth morning, looked likely to achieve
the impossible – a fourth-innings total of 479. All about
him his players reacted to mounting tension in predictable
ways. But Congdon sat there reading. This ability to
'switch off' has helped to take a good cricketer into the
ranks of the great.

'Many captains are not good watchers in tight situa-
tions,' said Congdon, in the dry, practical way which has
been a principal asset in newspaper and TV interviews.

'I read the book because I am a realist,' he said. 'Either
we would win, or we wouldn't. A lot of worrying will not
help your side to play better. Tension does not help. I base
my game on keeping it as simple as I can, and not allowing
tension to come into it in any circumstances.'

Congdon has become singularly successful in the art of
relaxation. Between deliveries in Test matches he looks at
advertisements, or he watches an aircraft fly by, studies the
crowd – anything to keep him from thinking about the ball
just bowled, the stroke just made.

'If you forget about everything that has gone before, it
lets you concentrate on what is coming,' he said. 'When I
relax out there, it might give the impression that I am
weary, but it is the way to rest. I did not feel exhausted, or
even tired, during the long innings at Trent Bridge and
Lord's. I pace myself fairly well.'

He needs to. In the Nottingham Test he was run out for 9
after batting for 40 minutes with an aplomb and certainty

Bevan Congdon

quite out of keeping with the desperate situation developing for his team. In the second innings he was in for nearly seven hours for 176, as fine a fighting innings as any played in Test cricket. At Lord's he applied himself diligently to getting his side into a winning position, batting over eight and a half hours for 175.

For sheer determination this lean, brown 35-year-old is almost in a class of his own. He is as fit and active as most players ten years his junior. But for all his practical ways, for all his successes, there is an appealing deference about him. Between his first Test series, in the New Zealand season of 1964–65, and New Zealand's visit to the West Indies last year, Congdon was regularly but not spectacularly successful. He had made a modest start, and then, after 31 Test matches, he had scored 1559 runs at an average a little above 26. In his five Tests in the West Indies and his next two overseas Test matches – Trent Bridge and Lord's – he made 891 runs at a Bradmanesque average of 99. He was asked to account for the very considerable flood tide of his cricketing fortunes:

'I think I learned quite a bit through batting for long periods with Glenn Turner,' he replied. 'I am probably adopting a slightly more professional approach now. I think perhaps my footwork has improved because I try to give myself as much time as I can, when the ball is in the air, before committing myself to a shot. Before, I think, I tended to make an involuntary movement one way of the other. Now I try to see line and length before I commit myself, and have a clearer decision to make.'

Bevan Congdon is the youngest of six brothers, all of them interested in cricket; but at 16 he almost gave cricket away in favour of tennis. He had enjoyed junior cricket in Motueka, a town in the northern part of the South Island. Motueka is renowned, in New Zealand, for sunshine, fruit, hops, and tobacco-growing. Now it is renowned for Congdon. He rejected tennis, although he had felt that being asked to play senior cricket at 16 would not bring the pleasure the game had given him earlier.

He was 24 before he played first-class cricket. A country player in New Zealand has to be exceptionally good to attract much attention. But Bevan Congdon, in his twenties, found ambition burning within him. He won a place in the Nelson Hawke Cup team, had a good first season, and so was selected for Central Districts in the Plunket Shield contest. He has never looked back. Now he has more runs in New Zealand cricket than anyone save John Reid and Bert Sutcliffe.

He has learned much – to discard, for instance, the sweep shot which cost him innings for a year or two; to bat out periods of good bowling, so he can survive for another spell of batting plenty. He is no Trumper, but Congdon today is an attractive batsman to watch. Patient, to be sure, but the strokes are there, and they are made when they are most likely to show a profit. At Lord's it was splendid to see his certain advance down the pitch to drive the slow bowlers.

His contribution to the success of the New Zealand tour this summer is almost immeasurable. He has been an iron man, unbending in his defiance of England bowling. He very nearly led England's little brother in Test cricket to two remarkable successes.

He is a remarkable man. Sometimes, it seems, his world is limited by the extremities of the pitch, and the man with the ball in his hand. This extraordinary application, and skills developed and matured by the years, have taken New Zealand cricket to a new height. And they have given Bevan Congdon a place all his own.

*When he was replaced by Glenn Turner as New Zealand's captain after the 1974–75 Tests against England, Bev Congdon had made 2911 runs and taken 51 wickets in his 50 Tests, and had led his country to an historic victory over Australia at Christchurch – a deed which gave him particular delight. The win at Christchurch will serve as some compensation for the near-misses in 1973 at Trent Bridge and Lord's. Against India in 1976 he was once more among the runs and wickets, and became only the second New Zealander to make 3000 runs in Test cricket.—Ed.*

# ROHAN KANHAI

## by Trevor Bailey

*The Cricketer* September 1973

Rohan Kanhai is not only one of the world's finest batsmen to come from West Indies, but he is also one of the most exhilarating, an artist with more than a touch of genius about his work. A Guyanan of Indian extraction, there is always some Eastern flavouring in his batting, especially in the more delicate of his strokes, like the late cut.

I will remember Rohan more for the way he made his runs than for the runs themselves; like the time he was playing for the Rest of the World against England and picked up a highly respectable ball from Tom Cartwright on about the leg stump and deposited it over the top of the long-on stand. It was a perfect example of both his ingenuity and the surprising power that he can put into his strokes, despite his slight, almost delicate build.

On one occasion in a Test I sent down a delivery which was just short of a length, but straightened off the pitch sufficiently to worry most players; but not Rohan. He simply adjusted his forcing back stroke and by angling his bat caressed the ball past cover's left hand to the boundary.

As with all great players Rohan has a sound technique to back up his very extensive repertoire of attacking shots. In his early days some of these were almost too extravagant and he is certainly the only person I have seen frequently hit a ball over the square-leg boundary with a cross between a pull and a sweep and finish up lying on his back. His magic stems from a wonderful eye, lightning reflexes, footwork, and perfect timing. He has the ability to take an attack apart with a savage yet essentially civilised assault, but he also possesses the skill, the defence, and the concentration to make a five-hour Test century.

Rohan's long and distinguished career as an international cricketer is best divided into four distinct phases,

152

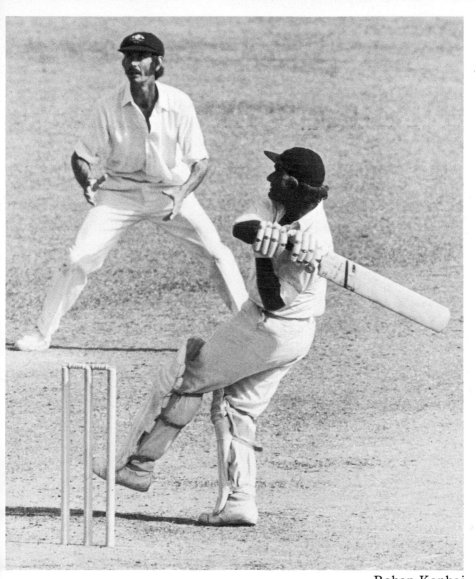

Rohan Kanhai

the novice, the flashing meteor, the mature craftsman, and captain of the West Indies. It was back in 1957 that he made his first trip to England with a West Indian side that never played to its potential and was heavily crushed in the Test matches. In those days he was a batsman of obvious promise and a wicketkeeper of rather less. Although he was clearly not as good as Gerry Alexander behind the stumps, he did keep in the first three Tests, and played as a batsman in the remainder.

On this tour there was no disguising his potential, but he was never given a settled niche in the order, opened on occasions, and had to be content with several flashing forties.

Rohan established himself as a world-class player when West Indies visited India and Pakistan. He proceeded to score more runs than anyone else, including double-centuries, with a brilliance and inventiveness often breath-taking. Any remaining doubts as to his rating among the truly great was finally dispelled during Frank Worrell's epic tour to Australia. It was Rohan who first caught the imagination of the Australian public with a flowing century against an Australian XI and followed it up with an even more remarkable double-century in Melbourne. Throughout the Tests he was the leading scorer and enchanted everybody with the splendour of his strokes. This represented the zenith of his power and from then, until phase three, the dazzling meteor sparkled only inter-mittently and he began to slide from real greatness to become just another, better than average, Test cricketer. This was typified by his rather laboured century in the final Test against England during his third visit to this country.

By 1968 Rohan could be said to have reached the cross-roads of his career. There were many who felt that he was finished at the highest level, but he was to prove them all wrong with an outstanding series against England in the Caribbean, a renaissance which proved to be as com-plete as Tom Graveney's. Nothing was more impressive than the way he withstood a barrage of speed in the West Indies first innings at Sabina Park on a pitch where the ball behaved unpredictably. His technique in stopping the shooter and the impressive manner in which he accepted the physical battering provided an exhibition of batting skill and courage.

This Kanhai comeback was largely due to a gradual change in outlook, because the ability was always there. Originally his character, like his batting, was inclined to flashes of impetuosity, but he grew up and matured. This enabled him to rethink and to control the occasional outburst both on and off the field. A wiser, more tolerant, and more generous person emerged to delight cricket-lovers everywhere.

Apart from Test cricket Rohan joined Warwickshire, where he has been an enormous success in every respect and his batting was one of the main reasons why his adopted county carried off the Championship.

The final accolade to a wonderful career occurred last winter when the greying, heavier, but still very active senator of West Indian cricket was invited to captain his country against the Australians. I thought he did well in the first Test at Sabina Park, which I saw, but subsequently it is reported that he became rather over-defensive and the Australians finished comfortable winners.

Now he is leading West Indies in England and in the first Test his side cruised to that victory which has eluded them for so long. One of the main reasons for this win was the shrewd and positive way he handled his team. In addition to being a master batsman and a fine slip he has developed into a very astute skipper, his performance at The Oval providing a classic exhibition of the art of captaincy.

*After the successful Prudential World Cup competition, there was no room for the veteran Rohan Kanhai in West Indies' side in Australia, even though he finished 1975 top of the national batting averages with 1073 runs at 82.53. All through the year there has been no escaping the fact that here was still one of the world's great players. A year earlier he had scorched to 213 not out in adding a world record 465 unfinished second-wicket partnership with Jameson for Warwickshire v Gloucestershire at Edgbaston. The charitable will remember these glories at the expense of the unpleasant exchanges on the same ground in 1973 when, as captain, Kanhai showed dissent when England's Boycott was given 'not out' after an appeal for 'caught behind'. At 40 Kanhai is playing club cricket in Melbourne and may well make many more runs for his English county.—Ed.*

# DEREK UNDERWOOD

## by Robin Marlar

*The Cricketer* October 1973

Derek Underwood is one of the larger gold nuggets on the cricket scene. As a cricketer he fascinates me. He is a phenomenon among bowlers. There is seldom more than one of those in a cricketing generation.

Our story begins, as Frankie Howerd might say, on a summer's day in 1945. The young Underwood, sired by a keen right-handed fast bowler christened Leslie Underwood, was born in Bromley 367 days after D-day. Sociologists would immediately park this young Underwood in the opening phase of the post-war bulge. The cricket boom which reached its peak in 1947 was due to begin. At the right moment a concrete wicket appeared in the Underwood garden: there was one in the garden of the young Frank Hayes, too. Concrete wickets in gardens make better grounding for young batsmen and fast bowlers than for spinners – but more of that later.

Derek Underwood duly arrived at the Dulwich College Preparatory School. He took nine wickets in an innings before he was 10; there's no experience like that for making a young bowler realise what is *possible* in cricket. For, ever after, eight or nine wickets in an innings represents a key to a private Shangri-La. If he enjoys visits to that special place, a bowler needs no other motivation. He is a bowler who has *bowled a side out*. Different. Formidable. A bigger figure in the side. Soon after, Underwood, now at Beckenham Grammar School, made 96 against the staff. Perhaps it was as well that he stuck to hitting wickets and not runs. He had developed a pair of bowler's 'plates'. That's what I remember best about his first season in the Kent side. He was 17. His feet were enormous. Great splayed members encased in heavy boots. To a Sussex man they looked especially ominous. They were Maurice Tate's feet.

In that season, 1963, Underwood bowled 950 overs and took 100 wickets at 21 apiece. There will never be a debut like it. And this comet blazed on and on. He had taken 1000 wickets before he was 26: only Rhodes and Lohmann reached that mark earlier in life. The 1000-wicket men are giants each and every one. In 1966 he became a Test cricketer. In 1968 he won a match against Australia: 7 for 50 in 31 overs at The Oval. He took the last wicket six minutes from the end. It was John Inverarity's. The ball pitched outside the off stump and would have hit. Inverarity was the last of three leg-before decisions Underwood got that day.

It was at about this time that cricket was beginning to come out of its worst-ever decade. One of the principal activities of this dark age was law-meddling. Under the new leg-before Law Inverarity would not have been out unless he had played no stroke. To get a leg-before decision Underwood – left-arm round – had to pitch on the wicket and hit it. On a good wicket this was nigh impossible. Claude Lewis, the Kent scorer, thought Underwood, England's best bowler, ruinously affected. Most Law-meddlers think like batsmen and are unaware of the mental effect of change on bowlers: the new Law restricted Underwood's target area and hence his effectiveness.

Up to that time he was comfortably averaging a wicket every ten overs. Since then he has been pushing towards eleven overs. But he has continued to be a star among bowlers, and though Norman Gifford edged him out of the England XI on numerous occasions during the Illingworth regime Underwood remained the favourite of most critics simply because of his *matchwinning* capability.

There are two other reasons for the clouding of his early glory. Batsmen, pressed by the needs of one-day cricket, are prone to lay back their ears at the sight of any bowler slower than fast-medium. A left-hander is fair game for the cross-bat swing to leg. No longer can he operate with a weakened leg side on a good wicket. Being swung to leg unhinges confidence. Underwood, who learned the steadiness any seamer must have on his concrete wicket, was uncannily

Derek Underwood

accurate in his late teens and early twenties. Hardly anyone got after him. Recently batsmen have sought to and sometimes succeeded in hitting him out of the firing line.

The second reason that life has become harder is that people now understand Underwood. As a world-class bowler with ten years' exposure he is revealed as a slow-medium to medium-pace left-arm bowler, primarily round the wicket, who can vary his pace, swing the ball in to the right-hander, occasionally make it leave the bat either off the seam or by finger cut, and – on a helpful wet wicket – make the ball rear to the point of being unplayable. In such conditions many sides – perhaps most of all New Zealand – have been annihilated. He is *not* a spin bowler as the ancients would understand the term. Spin bowlers are best reared not on concrete but on grass where they can see what happens when the ball is spun. It pitches and leaps off in another direction. The spun ball is the fun ball. A luxury.

Derek Underwood has the action of a medium-pacer. It is a fine action. Rhythmic. Controlled. Plenty of body. It lends itself to accuracy. He also has stamina. He can bowl for hours. But now he knows that this is not enough. To be as great a bowler in cricketing annals and affections as Wilfred Rhodes or Jim Laker or even Bishan Bedi he has to be able to get wickets all over the world and not primarily in England, the seamer's paradise. What is he to do? Is he to change his action and become a spinner, pure and simple? Or is he to develop another action and operate in two distinct styles? Who will teach him to spin the ball? 'This is a tricky one,' said another admirer, Colin Cowdrey. 'At this level we're talking about John Jacobs putting Tony Jacklin right.' Could Jim Laker do it? Someone must. Underwood has at least eight more years in which to play a vital part in winning a series on hard wickets overseas where the only aids are bounce and dust.

It will not be easy. Unlike some of the great non-spinning leg-spinners like O'Reilly, or the quicker off-break bowlers like Bob Appleyard – another fascinating operator – Derek Underwood has a slow arm action. Appleyard, like Laker, had a fast arm. So did Tom Goddard. So did Tony Lock, especially when he had the extra degree of devastation from a bent elbow. Lance Gibbs has a quick arm. From a fast arm all excellence in spin bowling derives: both the spin and the flight. Without a fast arm a spinner is plain. Batsmen can measure the minimal risk he is likely to pose and attack without fear or folly. At present Derek Underwood is trying to experiment but he has not yet achieved the breakthrough. I wish him well. If he were ever to succeed to the point of bowling a side out by flight and spin a second Shangri-La would be revealed. And that will be a priceless bonus for hours of work on the rebuilding of an action. The downside risk is enormous: suppose that he lost even that which he has in a fruitless search for something better. His character as well as his cricket is under test.

*The dissatisfaction, justified or not, surrounding Derek Underwood continues. In 1974 he routed Pakistan on damp Lord's wickets with 5 for 20 and 8 for 51. At Adelaide in January 1975 he took five Australian wickets before lunch on the first morning on a moist pitch. During the ill-fated Headingley Test later that year he took his 200th Test wicket: it was his 57th Test. Still only 30, he has more prospect than anyone else of reaching the heady heights of statistical achievement attained by Trueman and Gibbs.—Ed.*

# GEOFF ARNOLD

## by Rex Alston

*The Cricketer* December 1973

Geoffrey Graham Arnold – 'Orse' to his Surrey team-mates, which could be a tribute to his capacity for work as well as to his parents' choice of initials – is a late developer in first-class cricket. After joining Surrey in 1962 and having his first game in 1963, he made sufficient progress to be picked for the Under-25 team to Pakistan in 1966–67.

In a Zone match there he made his highest score to date, run out for 71. Thereby hangs a tale. There had been words between him, the bowler, and Saeed Ahmed, the batsman. When it was his turn to bat, Arnold backed up too enthusiastically, so Saeed took the bails off. Arnold asked if this was a warning, and the answer was, 'No, I'm appealing.' So Arnold had to go and he has not yet surpassed 71.

He feels that given the opportunity he could be a genuine all-rounder. As proof, he cites his second Test, against Pakistan at The Oval in 1967 – 5 for 58 and 59 runs.

But misfortune in the shape of injuries kept him back for the next few years. He missed most of 1968 through a cartilage operation, played in only one Test in 1969 and did not reach his full potential till 1971, when he took 83 wickets to head the bowling averages and help Surrey win the Championship. In the Tests he got no further than twelfth man, but the arrival of the 1972 Australians gave him his big chance, and anyone who saw his opening spell on a dull Old Trafford day is not likely to forget it. In conditions ideal for swing and seam bowling he had Stackpole missed at slip off one ball, missed again in the slips off the next, off which Stackpole scored a single, and had Francis missed, again at slip, off the next – an unprecedented feat of unrewarded accuracy. A hamstring injury kept him out of the Lord's Test, where he would have been England's answer to Massie (16 wickets for 137), but by the

Geoff Arnold

end of 1972 he was the acknowledged fast-medium complement to the speed of Snow, and he has been a first choice ever since.

In the five series against Australia in 1972, in India and Pakistan 1972–73, and against New Zealand and West Indies in 1973 he took 64 wickets in only 16 matches, proof that he has reached the top as a leading exponent of the art of new-ball bowling.

He had tips originally from Peter Loader on how to hold the ball so that on pitching it would move either way dependent on the angle at which the seam hit the ground. He also had help from Alec Bedser on how to bowl the unplayable ball which swings in to the batsman and then leaves him off the pitch – Alec's famous leg-cutter. He reckons that most batsmen are more vulnerable on the off side, so he concentrates on and outside the off stump. As a result he has noticed that some batsmen when facing him are taking middle-stump guard.

For a bowler who is no more than fast-medium, why does he take a 25-yard run? 'So far I have found that this is the best way of getting the correct rhythm, without which I lose my accuracy. But I have not been too put out by cutting my run down on Sundays, and towards the end of last season I experimented with 20 yards.' That would cut 60 yards off each over, nearly a mile in an average day, with consequent saving of time and energy.

He has been training hard for the coming West Indies tour. He peddles away on his stationary bicycle in his garage, runs with Wimbledon and Guildford Football Clubs, plays weekend golf (handicap 12) and as the time approaches for departure he will be having regular indoor nets. As a result he maintains he will be as fit as anyone else when the tour starts, as befits an all-round games player who would still be playing football for Corinthian Casuals had not Surrey asked him to give up for fear of injury. At 29 he is at the peak of his career and his immediate object is to do well in West Indies; he will be disappointed if he doesn't go to Australia with the next England team.

A few statistical highlights. The day after he heard he had won his first cap against Pakistan in 1967, he took 8 for

41 against Gloucestershire – his best performance to date. He ranks his 6 for 46 against India in Delhi last winter, on a pitch normally unfriendly to a bowler of his type, his best analysis in a Test. He is still waiting for his first hat-trick. His nearest approach was for Surrey Second XI v Essex Second XI. He took two wickets in two balls and the man who came in to face the hat-trick ball was a young West Indian named Keith Boyce. He duly steered it straight to first slip, who dropped a sitter.

He confesses to being a bundle of nerves before a big match. But give him the new ball and all traces of nerves vanish as he concentrates on thinking out his opponent, who is probably as nervous as he is. He loves bowling and would go on all day if asked – a great asset to his captain.

*Geoff Arnold continues to be a bowler for English conditions. At Lord's in 1974 he (4 for 19) and Chris Old (5 for 21) demolished India for 42. During the previous winter in West Indies he had had barely any success, and a year later in Australia his performances were moderate. He did, however, take his hundredth Test wicket when he dismissed Greg Chappell at Sydney.—Ed.*

# JOHN JAMESON

## by Clive Taylor

*The Cricketer* January 1974

John Jameson is expressionless and big. Big in the way they used to call barrel-chested, which means that he looks as if he is permanently holding his breath. Put a black hat on his head to hide his neat wavy hair and he could pass for a strong-arm man for the Mafia.

He is one of those the chairman of selectors, Alec Bedser, must think about – even though he does not name him – when he repeats his lament about the damage imported cricketers are doing English cricket.

Last year Jameson, bereft of form and figuring with more success in the Warwickshire second eleven than the first, looked a failing figure. No batsman can afford a loss of form in a side where Kanhai and Kallicharran, two batsmen whose names are always shown in neon lights, are regular members and where Amiss and M. J. K. Smith, whose birth certificate stopped registering about ten years ago, are among the competing Englishmen.

Failure in that kind of company can be final.

In 1972 as MCC flew to India and Pakistan, Jameson, who had been fairly successfully introduced to Test cricket against India a year before, was left behind. His omission caused no argument. Indeed, his average of 19.73 from 32 innings was so depressing that there was talk among the players over their breaking-up drinks that autumn that he would be leaving Warwickshire. Somerset was mentioned.

This year Jameson scored almost two thousand runs, averaged 48.70, finished thirteenth in the first-class averages yet in fact was placed number four among Englishmen as the other nine were all overseas players (another fact that is no doubt filed and indexed in the mind of Bedser).

Incidentally, and purely for those who collect curiosities, one place below Jameson, born in Bombay,

John Jameson

was Cowdrey, who first took guard up the road in Bangalore.

The selection of Jameson for West Indies that resulted was immediately linked in most minds with that of Colin Milburn, who had made the same tour six years earlier with Cowdrey's side in a similar role – the violent player with a brutal approach to the new ball.

The comparison is not strictly accurate, but it is fair. Jameson is not as big as Milburn (and he is more muscular). Neither is he as good a player. Yet clearly the selectors had the same principle in mind when they selected them – that their aggression would give England the initiative.

Milburn never got into the Test side in West Indies although his unfailing good humour and his loyalty still made him one of the outstanding players of the party. His lack of success was not all that important because he was surrounded by Cowdrey, Graveney, Barrington, Edrich and Boycott. For those who have wept for English batsmanship in recent seasons this recognition of the decline between two tours of West Indies is a cause for further mourning.

But where Milburn then was expendable Jameson now is vital. In a team which has been in decline since the Ashes were won in Australia and whose confidence is wobbling after the traumatic experiences of this summer, the success of a batsman who stands up and hooks the opposing fast bowlers can be decisive.

Jameson, playing brutally, would not only lift his own side but would take a credit point or two away from a West Indies team who will now be a much tougher proposition than before their successes at The Oval and Lord's.

If West Indies attack England this winter as they did this summer, through their quick bowlers, then Jameson need not fear. His courage has never been in dispute. He cuts and hooks and drives willingly at anything of medium pace and above.

Less certain is his ability to cope with Gibbs and Inshan Ali, the little left-hander who bowls out of the back of the hand. Gibbs, with his bounce and persistence, knows about Jameson, his Warwickshire colleague – a fact that became obvious when he shackled him in the Prudential Trophy match at The Oval.

Yet there is consolation here too, for Jameson's most important season to date was 1971 when he played in two Tests against India and then struck the tourists for 231, his highest score, when they played Warwickshire at Edgbaston. Included in that party were Chandrasekhar, Bedi, Prasanna and Venkat, the same bowlers who caused England's batsmen such strife last winter.

Clearly then, Jameson, who has been learning the business of batting in first-class cricket for thirteen years, is not a limited player. It may be too that like many other players he will find the task of coping with slow bowling less taxing in the slower tempo of Test cricket than in the frenetic atmosphere of the one-day game where there is always a moral obligation to slog at anyone who bowls slow.

In any case he may never have to face an extended trial by slow bowling, not if Kanhai runs true to type as a modern Test captain. The fast bowlers now are court favourites.

At 32 Jameson is probably past worrying. If his recent career has proved anything it is that you just have to keep playing your own way. It is the only way to stay out of the madhouse.

*John Jameson was not to 'come off' in Test cricket, though his brave, bold approach lent excitement to his few, brief appearances. At Kingston his first ball, a Boyce bouncer, was mis-hooked for six over fine third man. In county cricket his batting remained a weighty attraction; Warwickshire became one of the best 'chasing' sides in the country. And in July 1974 he dominated a world-record stand of 465 for the second wicket with Kanhai against Gloucestershire, making 240 not out in 100 overs.—Ed.*

# DENNIS AMISS

## by Gordon Ross

*The Cricketer* February 1974

If one does tend to think of Warwickshire as the possible pioneers of overseas talent in County Championship
cricket, the thought should not be allowed to blur the
care taken at Edgbaston to find and nurture home-grown
material. The shining example, of course, is Dennis
Amiss. He made his first appearance on the County Ground
at the age of fourteen, playing in the final of the Docker
Shield, one of the largest schools league competitions in
the country. He created an immediate impact, and Warwickshire told him: 'Come back when you are fifteen.' He did,
and was taken on the staff. As most of the other young
players were eighteen, Leslie Deakins recalls having said:
'What do we do with a 15-year-old?' He was told: 'Don't
worry, he'll fit in.'

This 15-year-old youngster was then an all-rounder, a
right-handed batsman, bowling left-arm medium, but a
subsequent injury when playing football – he slipped a disc
in his back – restricted full movement in his bowling
action, and must, at the time, have hampered his overall
development; but that, and his other problems, are now a
thing of the past.

Dennis Amiss is now a mature Test cricketer, but only
after having come along a hard road. Jackie Stewart said
once on the Frost programme: 'You learn to win well only
after losing badly.' In other words, you are better at the top
if, in getting there, you have shrugged off constant adver-
sity. You are so much better equipped.

To the connoisseur, knowing how much inbred natural
skill Dennis Amiss possessed, it was always difficult to
appreciate just why his cricket didn't flow, and why he
seemed to have periods when he was battling with himself
even more than with the bowler. It appeared in the end that

Dennis Amiss

putting him in first was a crucial turning point, but he feels himself that the root of the trouble lay in his own striving for a technical perfection, because he was conscious of the fact that he did not play back very often – he moved across his crease rather more than back. He went into the nets to try and put this right, but in truth, it was not an imperfection, and in the end Dennis realised that the way he played his cricket was something which had been built in over the years, and he was only getting himself into deeper water by trying to change it. He reverted to being Dennis Amiss again. This, and the stroke of genius of putting him in first, have together produced an England cricketer of rich qualities.

He felt that the winter tour of India and Pakistan gave him a new dimension. With only sixteen players, living, sleeping and eating cricket, and with only one or two likely candidates to get your place in the side, allied to the fact that pressures of Press and television are much less than in England, Dennis found a new and invigorating confidence.

Unlike Arthur Morris, who used to be known as Alec Bedser's 'bunny', or Keith Miller, who always had immense problems with Jim Laker on a turning wicket (but then who didn't!), Dennis has no qualms about any particular bowler. 'It all depends on the wicket,' he says, and he rates the best innings he ever played as when he scored 90-odd on a shaven wicket at Gravesend with Derek Underwood making the ball do everything but talk. It was a battle of wits, skill and temperament from the word 'Go'.

Dennis, in gratitude, talks of Derief Taylor, who began coaching him at the tender age of eight and who, he believes, practises the only philosophy for a good coach. He brings out what you have got. He does not try to put in what you have not. He is a quiet man but makes each of his pupils feel that he is an individual – no assembly-line techniques producing automation cricketers. Dennis also speaks of his father, a good club cricketer, who stimulated his early interests in the game of cricket.

He is a batsman whose repertoire includes the full range of strokes, though some say he has a slight hankering for the on side, and when he is going well he can bring back fleeting memories of the greatest on-side player since the war – Peter May. Yet to a major extent the bowler decides where you will play the ball – anything pitched on the leg stump can hardly result in a cover drive except with a great risk of faulty execution.

He has a natural eye for a ball game, though he keeps his golf very much in perspective and doesn't take it too seriously. After trying to thump a golf ball as far as he can down the fairway, it does tend to make him want to knock hell out of a cricket ball, and this could be good, bad, or indifferent, depending upon the situation at the time.

Born in the very heart of Birmingham, Dennis made his debut for Warwickshire in 1960 at the age of seventeen, but it was not until 1965 that he won his cap. In the following year he was picked for England for the fifth Test against West Indies at The Oval – a memorable game in which Graveney and J. T. Murray hit hundreds, and Higgs and Snow put on 128 for the last wicket. Amiss scored 17 before being leg-before to Wesley Hall. England won by an innings so that his performance was restricted to one knock, but it was the start, a slippery slope which he was to finally scale with courage, determination and distinction.

If we are to assess his batting in statistical terms alone, then there is much to record. Centuries in Test, county and Gillette Cup cricket – only eight runs short of a double-century against Lancashire in 1972, a couple of Gillette Man of the Match awards, a Benson & Hedges Gold Award, and also – he hopes you will notice – three wickets for 21 against Middlesex at Lord's in 1970; the victims of this assault were Radley, Murray and Titmus, a pretty useful triumvirate. Batsmen often look with affection upon their bowling performances as Norman Wisdom might hanker after playing Hamlet.

Now, seven years after his first meeting with West Indies at The Oval, Dennis Amiss takes them on again, on different terms, on wickets which should suit him admirably, and with a wealth of life's priceless asset behind him – experience. His place on the England side on this tour should never be in doubt   he's too good a cricketer now. A lot of water has flowed under the bridge since this small figure presented itself at the Thwaites Gates in 1958 to seek fame as a cricketer; now he has found it; none deserves ultimate success more than he.

*Runs continued to flow prolifically from Dennis Amiss's bat with almost unequalled regularity until the series in Australia in 1974–75. A year earlier, in West Indies, his 262 not out – one of the great endurance performances in cricket history – saved England at Kingston after his 174 in the first Test had merely postponed defeat. Another century followed at Georgetown, pursued by scores of 188 against India and 183 against Pakistan in the home series. When he was dismissed for 90 at Melbourne on the last day of 1974 he was two runs short of Bob Simpson's record Test aggregate (1381) in a calendar year. Glory was followed by grief. Amiss's scores against Australia thenceforth were 12, 37, 0, 0, 0, 4, 5, 0, 10, punctuated by a century in New Zealand. The general view, all the same, seems to be that it is unlikely that this batsman of contrasts will never play again for England.—Ed.*

# GLENN TURNER

## by Michael Melford

*The Cricketer* March 1974

In 1971 I found myself flying one morning from Auckland to Sydney in the company of the Australian crew returning home from competing in the One-Ton Cup. Yachtsmen, I concluded after having a good look at them, were picked not only for their physique but for their glamorous exterior and, sitting among these bronzed, muscular film stars, any one of them a strong contender for the next Tarzan epic, I felt somewhat out of place, not least because of the final savage assault of Auckland hospitality suffered the night before.

I was about to close my eyes on this aggressive show of robust health when among the smart uniforms of blue blazers, blue ties, grey flannel trousers and short haircuts, I noticed another intruder, slight, pale and in marked contrast with the Tarzans in every way. It was Glenn Turner, on his way somewhat improbably to play cricket in Kuwait – or was it Bahrain? – and as I lay back again, I pondered, with such concentration as I could muster, the diversification of talents among the human race.

This unassuming, relatively unathletic young man, then 23, had already performed some sporting feats beyond the scope of most mortals. He had carried his bat through a Test innings at Lord's, set a new Worcestershire record of ten hundreds in a season and in the previous English summer had scored 150 runs more than any other batsman in the country. Still to come, of course, was the scoring of 1000 runs by the end of May, a feat which no batsman had been expected to have the chance, let alone be good enough, to do again.

Glenn Turner's success is based inevitably on a sound method. He plays very straight, is a quick judge of length and a beautiful timer who can drive and play square on the off side with a power out of all proportion with his slender frame. In the last ten years I can recall two outstanding innings on turning pitches. One was by Dennis Amiss in Rawalpindi in March 1973, the other was by Turner in the less exotic and less turbulent surroundings of Welling-borough School in 1970. Worcestershire needed 225 in the last innings, which in the context of pitch and previous play, should have been well beyond them, but Turner made 110 not out with great skill and they won comfortably.

Dunedin, with its almost Scottish-type climate, is not the normal breeding-ground for a great batsman and a young New Zealander starts with none of the confident expectation of success of a young Australian batsman. Yet when I first saw him in Wellington, Turner had been picked as a promising 18-year-old for the President's XI against Mike Smith's MCC side. He had averaged over 50 for Otago in the Plunket Shield and though on this occasion he was lbw to Peter Parfitt for five, the selection in itself was an event in a land where batsmen tend to take quite as long to reach maturity as in England.

But at that time New Zealand cricket had an even greater sense of inferiority than usual and it is hard to believe that Turner would have become the batsman he is if he had not decided to come to England. The link between Dunedin and Edgbaston was an obvious one, for at the time of Mike Smith's visit Billy Ibadulla was coaching in Dunedin, and eventually, because Warwickshire could accommodate no more overseas players, Turner came to Worcester.

However much natural talent a batsman may possess there comes a point when his success depends on how much he makes of that talent. Temperament has probably played a bigger part in Turner's success than most. One obstacle which he has had to overcome is the traditional doubt at home about the local boy who wins fame overseas. When he went back to New Zealand in 1970, too much was expected of him and he had a modest season, so modest that on their arrival Ray Illingworth's MCC side were astonished to hear suggestions that he might not be in the Test team. He was, of course, picked and did fairly well, though the Auckland Test, which New Zealand

Glenn Turner

might have won, provided a sample of that strokelessness which sometimes shackled him. His opening stand of 91 with Graham Dowling took over three hours and on a superb pitch lost New Zealand the initiative on the second day.

One tended to forget that he was still only 23 and was not always sure enough of himself, especially perhaps in New Zealand, to play all the strokes within his range.

However, through the years this has been overcome to the benefit of Worcestershire and New Zealand and I should have thought that few innings by Glenn Turner are a hardship to watch nowadays. Perhaps the most convincing proof of the part played by an equable temperament is the way in which he kept going under pressure to achieve his two most famous feats.

In the last match but one of the 1970 season, against Lancashire at Worcester, he needed one more hundred for the Worcestershire record and, playing beautifully, he reached 99 in the second innings as the declaration was imminent. At this point the Lancashire captain set a field with only one man in front of the wicket on the off side, inviting Turner to take a single there and expedite the declaration. Turner duly tapped the ball on the off side and ran. By some oversight, however, Clive Lloyd had been left as the lone fielder there and, swooping like some great black hawk, he threw Turner out at the bowler's end. Run out 99, a few inches from a historic achievement! It was a cruel blow.

But Turner was undeterred, even by a lively pitch at the start of his innings in the final match, against Warwickshire, and he made 133. In much the same way three seasons later he reached 1000 runs on May 31 by reaching 93 on a far from perfect pitch when for some days the target had seemed to be escaping him.

Runs are not everything – how and where they are made is usually what matters – but this feat, as Walter Hadlee said, would capture the imagination of schoolboys at home and have beneficial effects for the future of New Zealand cricket. Thus, although Glenn Turner's career is still young, its impact is already considerable.

178

*Glenn Turner's greatest moment came at Christchurch in March 1974 when he made 101 and 110 not out against Australia in New Zealand's historic five-wicket victory, which was all the more satisfying for Turner since he had been the target of 'verbal aggression' from the opposition. In the Prudential World Cup he averaged 297 in three innings (two not-out) in the preliminary matches, but was unable to lead his side past the semi-final against West Indies. He had a quiet year with Worcestershire in 1975, though topping their averages. Leading New Zealand against India in 1976, he scored his sixth Test century in the second match. He should put many thousands more runs into the book during the 'seventies.—Ed.*

# G. R. VISWANATH

## by K. N. Prabhu

*The Cricketer* May 1974

The domestic season of 1968–69 was a dismal one. India were smarting from successive defeats inflicted on them by England in the summer of 1967 and by Australia that same winter. Many among the Old Guard had retired. Rusi Surti, who had had a successful tour, stayed behind in Brisbane. Farokh Engineer had migrated to England. Borde was on the decline. Only Pataudi remained to make cricket live and challenging.

That season, having watched Bombay carry all before them in the Ranji Trophy, I ventured south to see what the other Zones had to offer.

It was a rewarding trip. For I saw in Gundappa Raghunath Viswanath, to give him his full name, an India batsman in the making. Playing for Mysore against Hyderabad he made about forty runs. It was a short, neat innings, but the manner in which he faced the Hyderabad spinners and the strokes he bared to view set him apart from the common run of batsmen. He was then just twenty years of age.

On my return to headquarters I wrote a piece on him. But the cynics were sceptical. They preferred to reserve judgment to an occasion when Viswanath would be tested against the best bowling in the land. Ironically, the best bowling in the land, Chandra and Prasanna, played for Viswanath's own State, Mysore.

That year Viswanath's name cropped up several times in the scores of matches held in aid of various causes. And they were made against the best bowlers in the land. But our selectors, in all their wisdom, were not inclined to test him when the chance came against New Zealand the following season – though he played a classic innings of 68 for the Board President's XI against the tourists at Indore.

180

G. R. Viswanath

The critics, as usual, were inclined to point to his weakness. He was said to have too high a backlift. He was believed to be fallible to the outgoing ball. I wonder how many batsmen in the world have claimed to master the outgoing ball?

But Viswanath took all this criticism with philosophical resignation. After all, hadn't he been rejected by the All-India Schools selectors on account of his height! That selection committee was apparently presided over by men who, like Frederick of Prussia who recruited his bodyguard from the tallest men in Europe, believed that height is all!

But the Indian Test selectors eventually had to bow to public opinion. That same winter, after the New Zealanders had left, Viswanath got his chance against Bill Lawry's Australians. In the second Test at Kanpur he scored a duck but he came back to make 137.

He acknowledges his debt to the Nawab of Pataudi, who gave him the necessary confidence. When he failed 'Pat' encouraged him with: 'Don't worry, you'll get another chance.'

'Vish' said afterwards: 'I got it in the same match and grabbed at it.' For Alan Connolly, who had tested him with bouncers, now found him hitting back with the hook. Eventually Viswanath finished the series with an average of 43.

Since then, Viswanath has known the ups and downs that are part of cricket. He has taken them as part of the glorious uncertainties – with his typical earthy humour – ever ready to join in a laugh at his own expense, whether it be in his attempts to talk pidgin hindi (the national language) or English. He found it especially funny at Birmingham to measure his 5ft 4½in against that of the giant Dunkels, of Warwickshire.

In West Indies Viswanath was bothered by a knee injury he had sustained during a trial game before the tour. But he showed enough of his class for Sobers, who observed him at close quarters, to rate him as a better batsman than Gavaskar.

In the English summer of 1971 he began with a flourish

with two centuries in a row, followed by an innings of 90 against Warwickshire. He made 946 runs at 41 on the tour, only 128 of them in the three Tests, where, apart from a knock of 68 in the Lord's Test, the big scores eluded him – as they did against Lewis's team last winter.

The wristy square cut was his strength as well as his weakness. He was on the verge of being dropped for the final match of the series when he scored an unbeaten 75 in the drawn Test at Kanpur.

He was to expose the selectors in the final Test when he made 113 – full of wristy drives, square cuts and thrusts to mid-wicket. Incidentally, he broke a hoodoo – as no other who had achieved a century in his first Test for India had managed to score another.

India's batting on this coming tour will depend heavily on Viswanath and his team-mate from Mysore, Brijesh Patel. Both, in full cry, are a treat to watch. Both are excellent fielders in the deep. Viswanath will have the company he needs, but even on his own, Viswanath can be trusted to enjoy his cricket and entertain those who watch him.

*'Vishy' is second only to Gavaskar for consistency among the current Indian Test batsmen. In the difficult series against England in 1974 he returned 40, 50, 52, 5, 28 and 25, some of his innings being played in conditions hardly conducive to success even by batsmen of full stature. As expected, he was a principal attraction during India's 1976 tour of New Zealand and West Indies, having made 139, his highest Test score, against the latter at Calcutta in 1975.—Ed.*

# BERNARD JULIEN

## by Colin Cowdrey

*The Cricketer* June 1974

Bernard Julien can thank the Duke of Norfolk for enabling him to leap over the final hurdles to the top so speedily. His tour of the Caribbean in 1969, which I was privileged to captain, took in Trinidad and we saw young Julien in one of his early matches. With the blessing of Leslie Ames and the Kent committee I invited him to join us at Canterbury that summer. It was to be a year of qualification, a taste of English conditions in our second eleven and a valuable education for him. First the seed and then the blade and then the full corn on the ear. What fun it has been for Kent to see this fine young cricketer develop and mature.

He comes from a family who love cricket and was put on the right road, too, by various splendid cricketers in Trinidad like Jeff Stollmeyer, Gerry Gomez, Charlie Davis, Joe Carew, not forgetting the Island coach at that time, Wesley Hall.

Bernard Julien is a superb athlete. When he is in full flow, batting, bowling or fielding, there is something of Sobers about him – the sheer rhythm and music of cricket oozes through every pore. He catches the eye and, like the top artist, he has the gift of radiating pleasure.

As a 13-year-old he was selected for the primary schools of Trinidad on a two-week tour of Barbados – his first real taste of competitive cricket. He scored 78 in one of the matches and was often in the wickets. Later, as a 16-year-old playing for St Mary's College, he scored 210 not out, a remarkable feat for a schoolboy. Within a couple of years he was playing in a first-class match for the North $v$ South, taking a hat-trick with the new ball and finishing with 8 for 59 in the innings, having reverted to a slower variety.

When I first saw him he looked full of cricket but raw from the point of view of experience in match-play. He was to have an exasperating first summer with Kent, but he was

Bernard Julien

particularly lucky to have the wise and patient counsel of Colin Page, our second-eleven captain. He was fortunate, too, to benefit from the example of Kent's other overseas cricketers, Asif Iqbal and John Shepherd, two of the world's best ambassadors in sport. But for a long time he was something of an enigma. When he was good he was too good to be true, it seemed, but all too often he looked out of his depth. However, it ought to be said, in fairness to him, that it was a particularly unhappy time for him. Just before he came to England, he lost his father and with Trinidad in a state of upheaval he was very concerned at having to leave his mother at such a time.

1970 was his first full year with the county, a disappointing one but a vital year of apprenticeship, listening, learning and experimenting. There were many who doubted whether he would break through but by the end of 1972 the Kent public had warmed to his lovely smile and had begun to appreciate his rich talents. He was now firmly on his way to the top. I shall never forget the ninety he scored at Dover against Northants in as many minutes, truly brilliant batsmanship. I recall his winning the Man of the Match award in his first appearance in the Gillette Cup by taking 5 for 29 against Yorkshire at Canterbury. His prize scalp that day was Boycott. The measure of a good bowler is in the number of times he dismisses the best batsmen. In the eight Test matches he has played so far, he has got Boycott out five times.

His selection for the West Indies tour of England came as no real surprise but one could not help wondering whether, from his point of view, it had come a year too soon. I knew that he could hold his own as a bowler, and he is a fine fielder anywhere, but I feared that his batting technique needed tightening. I need not have bothered. In his second Test at Edgbaston he raced to 54 and then came the unforgettable hundred in a record partnership with Garfield Sobers before a full house at Lord's. What a proud day that was for Kent and Trinidad!

I think I can safely say that he is now an established West Indian Test cricketer in his own right at the age of 25. He has the prospect of a marvellous career ahead of him, proven in Test matches yet, at the same time, tailor-made for one-day cricket. He has a lovely physique, lissom yet immensely strong. He can throw as far as anyone and, as Dennis Amiss in the third Test match in Barbados will recall, he is a superb close catcher.

Behind a rather sleepy-looking poker face lies a heart of gold, an alert mind and a disarming sense of humour. 'I love a contest, a challenge,' he said to me. 'I love bowling against the best batsmen in the world; I love playing before large crowds; I love a tough match, yet I believe that cricket, like life, has to be for fun.'

'Would you like to captain Trinidad and then lead the West Indies team to England in five years' time?' I asked. Sheepishly, modestly, he gazed at me at some length and gave no reply, but those lovely white teeth and the twinkle in his eye left me in no doubt as to his final aspirations. He acknowledges that he has to bring more discipline to his game. If he can emulate his two distinguished seniors, Sobers and Kanhai, by doing that, I believe he has it in him to be the best of his generation.

Cricket thrives on players like Bernard Julien – he has so much to give – I hope he succeeds, for Kent, Trinidad and West Indies.

*Injury, the dread of all sportsmen, kept Bernard Julien out of cricket for many frustrating months, and the 1975–76 tour of Australia marked a return for him to full activity. He was not seen at his best during the Prudential World Cup. Still only 26 in 1976, he seems certain to make further deep impressions upon Test cricket.—Ed.*

# MIKE BREARLEY

## by Robin Marlar

*The Cricketer* July 1974

Mike Brearley is 32 now. Cricket, powerful attraction though it is, is lucky to claim him still. By his age many of those who worked the silver-spoon passage from school to Oxford or Cambridge and thence into cricket had either said goodbye or had some clear plans as to when they would. Peter May and Ted Dexter head the list of early retirements and only Colin Cowdrey, still wallowing happily and beautifully in the world he loves and graces, looks likely to last a full natural span.

Brearley has already made one break. Cricketers from universities do have a ration of grey matter, though Don Shepherd of Glamorgan used to say that you'd never think so from the way they played the game. Most have only modest claims to scholarship, however, and a Brearley or an Eddie Craig, first-class honours men, are apt to be regarded with awe in the dressing room at Fenner's. Ability as unusual as Brearley's is jealously nurtured in the academic greenhouse, especially if it shows signs of taking root.

Brearley was soon teaching philosophy to the under-graduates. For two seasons, 1966 and 1967, he did not play first-class cricket in England. His absence makes his 312 at Peshawar in the winter between those two seasons look a real condemnation of our cricket at that time. And, indeed, it was very bad. No other member of that Under-25 side made such an impression as the captain, whose role was almost that of the absentee landlord. He was as skilful off the field as on it. Peter Smith, who accompanied the team, recalls that when the players were showing signs of being over-curried, Brearley decided to test the system by order-ing steak-and-kidney pie, roast potatoes, cauliflower with apple pie and custard – and got the lot.

Mike Brearley

Mike Brearley came back to cricket because he 'didn't want to teach philosophy all his life'. He is still not sure what he wants to do next. For a time it worried him – but not now. Materially his needs are not great. His wife teaches English at a technical school. They have no children. He knows why he is playing cricket and why for the moment he wants to continue.

He admires craftsmanship in cricket: the craftsmanship of Tom Cartwright for instance, a man who has helped him to play better. 'Much of our coaching is lamentable – even coaches who know the game take too little account of the individual's needs.'

He wants to be a better batsman. He knows he has a restricted range of back-foot strokes – 'only the cut, and bowlers don't bowl for that' – so that short-of-a-length bowling presents him with difficulty. 'I am better organised now', and he cites a good season for Middlesex in 1973 with an average of 40 to prove it.

His other purpose is to enjoy the county captaincy, 'trying to do it as well as I can'. He is, as the son of a schoolmaster, devoted to passing on his knowledge to the younger players. 'Yet captaincy can be so frustrating – it would be nice to win something.' Outsiders must take the view that Middlesex in the mid-1970s no longer have the players for serious pot-hunting.

Are the problems of Middlesex going to thwart any further cricketing ambitions of Brearley? He accepts absolutely the current dogma that a captain, especially of England, has to be worth a place in the side. At one time he was more ambitious to play for England than he is now. But surely he was one of those in the selectors' eye, and is he not affected now because he is rather out of it? 'I felt when I was in the eye that they were casting round rather desperately. But of course I'd like to be good enough at both batting and captaincy to have a chance.'

Away from the game Brearley is a reader of novels, a theatre-goer, 'and I'd like to spend a lot of time in the South of France – who wouldn't?' He is also an accomplished writer on cricket – there is a splendid piece by him on the leg-side limitations in the TCCB booklet *Cricket '74*. 'I was going to write for the *Standard* again but the Union has stopped me from doing more than six pieces for them. I'd like to join the Union but I can't – journalism doesn't provide me with half my earnings and I'm not sure that I want to do it full-time.'

A man of many talents, Mike Brearley has chosen to live his life in cricket.

Whatever the crabbed may think and say there *are* still personalities in the game. He is one of the most interesting. Essentially rational, a balanced individual, he brings an unusual quality to our cricketing scene – the pursuit of a craft skill, batsmanship, by a man of outstanding intellect. And because of that intellect there are many mansions ahead to which he may yet travel and thereafter dwell with distinction.

His is a career to watch. As it unfolds it will be a commentary not only on J. M. Brearley the man but also on our society.

*Mike Brearley had a distinguished season in 1975, heading the Middlesex batting with 1656 runs at 53.41 (four centuries) in the County Championship and, more memorably, leading Middlesex not only to their first cup final at Lord's but two – the Benson & Hedges and Gillette – both of which were lost. With Greig's appointment, Brearley's name finally ceased to be spoken of as a possible England captain.—Ed.*

# INTIKHAB ALAM

## by Jim Laker

*The Cricketer* August 1974

One of the most controversial issues in English cricket over the past seasons centred around the wisdom or otherwise of the registration of overseas cricketers by the counties. Possibly one could make a decent case for the 'anti-brigade' in terms of certain counties where the progress of the younger English players may well have been retarded, but a criticism of this nature could never be levelled at the Surrey club when after a great deal of deliberation they finally decided to engage Intikhab Alam in 1969.

In this day and age there could never be any question about 'Inti' depriving some young promising leg-spinner of a place in the side nor could any of the regular capped players be alarmed that this engaging cricketer was to be paid a salary which might lead to any dissension in the camp. Intikhab was delighted to accept terms on a par with his team colleagues, and was overjoyed that at long last he was able to spend every day of the week doing exactly what he had yearned to do all his life – bowling leg-spinners. More than that I have always sensed that there was also a feeling of pride as he put on his pads, collected his gloves and bat, and pulled on the chocolate-coloured cap and made his way down the pavilion steps.

It is hard to discover any Pakistani cricketer without hereditary claims to represent his country and Intikhab is no exception. He was, in fact, born in India in the small rural town of Hoshiarpur in the East Punjab, one of three sons of Naseeruddin Khan, the chief erection engineer of a large company with British ties which was involved in the construction of power stations in the region. His father was both an enthusiastic and talented cricketer, a fast bowler who regularly played against Amarnath and leg-spinner Amir Elahi, and if he did not reach the heights of Test

Intikhab Alam

cricket, he must have been close to selection. The bitterness of Partition soon after the war saw the family fleeing to Pakistan and subsequently all three sons of Naseeruddin played first-class cricket.

Intikhab, in common with most youngsters, began his cricketing life as a medium-fast bowler, but on the advice of his brother Nasim he decided to switch to spin for Nasim had quickly come to the conclusion that there were greater opportunities and lesser competition for young 'Inti' if he could master the intricacies of leg-spin bowling.

He surely had a dedicated convert, for each and every day Intikhab would cycle the two miles to Jehangir Park and think nothing of bowling for two to three hours on end in the heat of the afternoon. He was fortunate to discover around this time that the tough texture of his skin provided him with few worries about splitting spinning finger calluses. I can seldom recall him in recent seasons suffering this way.

His first appearance in senior grade cricket in Karachi was something of a fluke for it was only on the advice of a friend that he was around to find a place in the Karachi Greens, who gained a convincing win over Karachi Whites, a side close to Test match standards. His long stints of serious practice paid dividends, and his five well-earned wickets put him within reach of the Test side, particularly as the ageing Amir Elahi was beyond his best.

So it was that at the tender age of 17 Intikhab was included in the Test squad when the West Indies arrived in 1958. He was wisely allowed to soak up the Test match atmosphere before being called upon to make his Test match debut against Richie Benaud's Australians the following year. He well merited his selection after collecting nine wickets for the President's XI at Rawalpindi. If ever there was a story-book debut in Test match cricket it surely belonged to him. Before a packed house on his home ground of Karachi the great Fazal Mahmood gave Intikhab an early opportunity with a fair amount of shine still on the ball. The batsman facing was as tough a competitor (as I know to my cost) that you could encounter – Colin

McDonald, who played 47 Tests as Australia's opener. Intikhab's first ball, his normal leg-break, pitched around off stump and McDonald anticipating the spin went for his favourite cut; but the ball skidded straight through and clipped his off stump. The cricket-loving Pakistani supporters had themselves a new overnight hero.

Thus began a Test career which has now taken Intikhab within close proximity of 100 Test wickets, a landmark he will surely reach during the coming months. He has already become the first Pakistani to take 1000 wickets in first-class cricket.

Captain of his country and vice-captain of the Rest of the World side are appointments of the greatest possible importance to Intikhab, but at the same time he will look back with great satisfaction upon the seasons he spent as professional in the West of Scotland. He had become a fine exponent of the art of leg-spin, top-spin and googly bowling on hard unfriendly wickets around the world but in the far north he quickly found it required a different technique to succeed on slow damp pitches against club cricketers with aggressive intent.

The period spent in Scotland made him into the complete cricketer and subsequently made it possible to adapt his style with bat and ball to fit Surrey's requirements for the various competitions which now embrace the cricket scene in this country.

He epitomises the new generation of Pakistani cricketers and if by chance on only one Test occasion this summer we should run across Sadiq, Mushtaq, Majid, Asif and Intikhab in full flow it will be an occasion to remember.

Possibly the last word should be left to Intikhab himself when he says: 'Cricket is a way of life. You learn so much. It is a great teacher and it makes you a real man. It taught me patience, understanding and determination. My motto is "Live for the People". It is the only way.'

*'Inti' took his hundredth Test wicket during the 1974 series in England, and led Pakistan in two further Tests at home against West Indies, being knocked flat by a bouncer from Roberts at Lahore. The national selectors then withdrew the*

*captaincy from him a second time and he missed the Prudential World Cup. He had a quiet 1975 season with Surrey, but may yet return to Pakistan's colours as that country tries to discard the dull cloak of drawn matches.—Ed.*

# JOHN EDRICH

## by Trevor Bailey

*The Cricketer* October 1974

Successful batsmen come in many shapes and sizes. Their methods may vary from the strictly functional to the romantic, but they all have one fundamental in common: runs. Over a period of five years they will inevitably score a vast number, including many centuries. In the case of a class international batsman, he will have a first-class batting average in the mid-forties, or above, and a Test average of over forty. A quick glance at the figures of John Edrich reveals that he is no exception.

To make runs in such profusion at this level a batsman requires more than mere ability. He needs a good temperament, the power to concentrate for long periods, a certain amount of physical courage, self-discipline, and, most important of all, determination. These five virtues have played a bigger part in taking John to the top of his profession than his natural skill with the bat. There have been many players with as much basic ability as John (or even more) who have failed to score half as many runs, let alone establish themselves as automatic choices for England.

I remember one cricketer who looked a god in the nets, yet never made any runs in the middle. There was another who was a brilliant strokemaker, but regularly returned to the pavilion after a bright twenty or thirty. Then there was the case of the overseas import who would murder bowling on good pitches, but was so frightened of pace that Fred Trueman only needed to scowl to have him tripping over the square-leg umpire. Many outstanding county players have simply been unable to reproduce their true form in Test matches, and I can think of another who simply had too many shots.

I first encountered John Edrich in the late 'fifties, when he had just become an opener for Surrey, and it was immediately obvious that he was destined for greatness.

His style was not particularly attractive, his technique far from copybook, and his repertoire of strokes comparatively limited; but his bat, from a bowler's angle, always appeared unpleasantly straight, and unnaturally broad. He plainly took his chosen trade very seriously, got right behind the line of the ball, was unworried if beaten, thrived on the difficult situation, and had the knack of churning out the runs.

John has the build of a typical scrum half, stocky and tough, with a prominent, pugnacious jaw, so often a feature of the Edrich clan. He looks what he is, a born fighter, who usually has to be dug out, the breed every captain wants in his side. It was this attribute which was largely responsible for his recall to the international scene this summer, when most people, including himself, thought that his distinguished Test career was over.

The Edrich pedigree is similar to that of the majority of class English professionals. He joined his county, Surrey, as an exceptional young cricketer in his teens. After a comparatively brief apprenticeship, he took over as opener in the first eleven for the most obvious of reasons, he consistently made runs. He would probably have arrived even sooner if it had not been for two years of National Service, and was capped for England on merit when he was 26.

John's approach to batting has been that of a realist. Over the years he has developed his own workmanlike style, which is instantly recognisable, and has proved to be admirably efficient and effective. Although he may occasionally indulge in the flamboyant, he is mainly an acquirer of runs, who has learned to play within his limitations.

His defence is solid, and, rather surprisingly for a small man, he plays largely from over the crease, or half-cock, seldom moving either forward or right back on to his stumps. As one would expect from a number one, he thrives on seam bowling and I detested bowling at him, despite normally fancying left-handers. In his early days I thought he appeared a shade vulnerable against wrist-spin, which, unless he was on the attack, he tended to play rather

John Edrich

diffidently from the crease. Like all the really sound bats his judgment of line and length is excellent, so that he knows instinctively what to leave alone.

John can naturally produce most of the shots, when he wants, but his two most productive, or bread-and-butter strokes, are the firm punch off the legs, which sends the ball in an arc between mid-wicket and fine leg, and a run down through the gully off a cleverly angled bat. The latter should not be confused with the unintentional edge. His very loose grip on the handle enables him to place his pushes and nudges with remarkable accuracy.

The pick of John's more spectacular strokes are a blistering cover-drive off the front foot, and a high, very powerful, lofted on-drive into the crowd, and much appreciated by them.

Although he has frequently acted as a sheet-anchor, both for Surrey and England, a role for which he is admirably equipped, it should not be thought that he is only a dependable grafter. He can gather his runs very quickly, as he demonstrated so well during the summer of 1965, which I have always thought of as his 'biff-bang' season. After a winter in South Africa, he decided to go for his shots and the result was an exciting flow of boundaries, including a remarkable number of sixes. Many bowlers wilted under this barrage, and he hit New Zealand for a treble-century which he considers his finest and certainly his most extravagant innings because everything he attempted came off. However, in the main, his Test hundreds, of which a quarter have so far been made against Australia – another indication of class – have been quieter affairs.

John, never a powerful driver off his back foot, prefers batting on fast pitches, where the ball comes on to the bat. This is one of the reasons why he has an especially distinguished record abroad, where these conditions are more common. Like all openers, and this also applies when he has gone in at No. 3 for England, he has had to face the best quick bowlers of the past fifteen years. Despite his lack of inches, and not being a serious hooker, he has coped remarkably well. He did suffer one horrid blow on the head from a Peter Pollock bouncer at Lord's which inevitably caused him to lose confidence for a year or so. However, this hard little man soon shrugged off this injury and is prepared to stand out there staunchly as the deliveries fly past his head, or drop off the deadest of bats, with just the occasional glare at the bowler.

No review of John's batting would be complete without a mention of his passion for the stolen single. His running between the wickets, especially with Micky Stewart, has always been a feature of his play, and a very rewarding one, which has been greatly assisted by the accuracy of his placements.

When after a series of low scores he lost his place in the national XI he was suffering from a surfeit of cricket and was beginning to lose appetite for both runs and the game itself. His appointment as captain of Surrey, viewed with a certain amount of sceptism in certain quarters, rekindled his interest and recharged his batteries. It took him about a year to settle down, but in 1974 I rated him the most improved skipper on the county circuit. Under his command Surrey had a very good season and nobody played a bigger part in winning the Benson & Hedges Cup than John because the match turned into a tactical battle between the two captains, and his opponent was none other than the redoubtable Illingworth! Surrey have improved their tight bowling and defensive field placings, so essential in the limited-overs game, and he thoroughly earned his appointment as vice-captain in Australia.

By nature John is a careful cricketer with a slightly pessimistic outlook which to some extent may be due to the Oval pitch, which has so often frustrated a definite result. Whereas Godfrey Evans would suggest that his side would get the runs tonight, which with five wickets down and 350 still required might be termed a shade optimistic, John is never really contented unless the opposition is all out. Even if they are 250 behind with nine wickets down, it still might rain! Beneath his quiet exterior lurks a marked sense of rather sardonic humour, which can be seen in his blue eyes, shining out from beneath heavily hooded brows to lighten and soften a strong, rather serious face.

*The legendary courage of John Edrich was again in evidence in Australia in 1974–75, when the Australian fast attack broke hearts as well as fingers. At Sydney, Edrich had two ribs cracked by a short ball from Lillee. Giving not an inch of ground, the 38-year-old then had an outstanding home series on slower pitches against the same tormentors, piling up 175 in the Lord's Test and, at The Oval, missing by four runs what would have been his eighth hundred against Australia.—Ed.*

# FRED TITMUS

## by Gordon Ross

*The Cricketer* December 1974

At a time when the principal subject of discussion among cricketers was the game's most complicated player (Geoff Boycott) and his withdrawal from the party to tour Australasia this winter, it was a breath of fresh air to be talking to the most uncomplicated cricketer of them all, Fred Titmus, who, when asked why it was he thought he had been chosen to tour at the age of 42 (he was 42 on November 24) replied simply and succinctly, 'Well, I suppose it is because I have just kept on bowling.'

Those few words are not the first that came into his head; they are a philosophy; they are, in essence, the way he plays his cricket, simply but effectively. Spin bowling is a subtle art of flight and turn, and variation of pace, but to a great extent dependent for its success upon the state of the pitch, and Titmus believes that the greatest single factor in the decline of the craft of spin is the pitches, which, largely because of the excess of top-dressing, have become slower and slower. 'I find I spend half my life bowling uphill these days,' he says; 'the pitches have been built up so much, and when you do get one that suits you, you need to be Derek Underwood's pace to take advantage of it, as the ball rarely flies, it dollies up instead.'

It is widely thought that one-day cricket has been the villain of the piece in the spin bowler's life. Titmus does not share this view. There was a phobia, he admits, among captains to rule out spin bowlers altogether when the Gillette Cup began; they were simply dropped from the side; time proved the error of these ways, and, except in the Sunday slog, the spin bowler can often be the most economical proposition; bowlers like Norman Gifford, Derek Underwood, David Hughes and Jack Simmons have, at times, proved worth their weight in gold.

How much does Fred Titmus study the strengths and

weaknesses of batsmen; not as much as many might imagine. 'It matters more what I am doing than what the batsman is doing. If I am bowling well, he can only hit me in certain directions, and I set a field accordingly. I like to feel that I am dictating what is happening, more than the batsman.'

Titmus is an interesting cricketer because in his early days he had precious little coaching. His idol was Denis Compton, but as a footballer, and it was only the fact that Denis played cricket as well that served to stimulate a passionate interest in cricket. When watching Middlesex, Titmus was fascinated by Jack Young, and likes to think that he is a right-handed version of him. In fact there was a time when he had that little hop in his run-up that Jack's did, though somewhere along the line Titmus lost it. Jack Young became his mentor, and what he said was canon law. He rarely told you how to bowl; he told you what to bowl.

Titmus feels that the players of his early days were more willing pupils of experience than they are, perhaps, today, though this is just a passing comment and not a condemnation. The discipline was more rigid, of course, especially if you happened to have Walter Robins as captain! . . . but you were all the better for it.

His selection for this tour was no surprise to the connoisseur; whatever his age may be, he just happens to be the best off-spin bowler in the country. Tours in the past have been crucial turning points in his career. On the 1962–63 tour of Australia and New Zealand he was one of the three off-spinners chosen, a selection pretty strongly criticised on the grounds of bad balance. The three were Allen, Illingworth and Titmus, with Titmus not expected to be the front-runner, but as events turned out, he was. He took 21 wickets in the Tests, one more than Trueman, achieved a batting average of 36.40, and was bracketed with Ken Barrington as the outstanding success of the tour. This established him as an England player and he has now played in 49 Test matches with the strongest possibility of more to come, when it had seemed in tragic circumstances that his Test career was at an end.

Fred Titmus

Having played in the first two Tests in West Indies in 1967–68, Fred Titmus was involved in a boating accident in Barbados which caused the loss of four of his toes on his left foot, which had become caught in the screw of a small boat, placed in the middle of the craft and, contrary to regulations, without a guard. He returned home with his future as a cricketer considerably in doubt, let alone as a Test cricketer. Ray Illingworth moved into the England side, was successful, and despite a remarkable recovery by Titmus, the place was never there for him again; but as he says himself, 'he just carried on bowling', and now with this fairy-tale ending.

E. M. Wellings wrote at the time: 'So, injury almost certainly ended the Test career of Titmus. A total of 1311 runs and 146 wickets are witness of the value to England of his gritty cricket. He scaled the heights during the 1962–63 tour of Australia and that of India a year later. Though suffering from nagging shoulder trouble, he still held his own in big cricket and was Cowdrey's vice-captain in West Indies.'

At school at the William Ellis School, Highgate, Fred Titmus made his debut for Middlesex in 1949 at the age of sixteen; his promotion from the ground staff to the Middlesex XI had a story-book touch about it. It happened in June, 1949 when Middlesex, with Robertson, Compton, Edrich, Mann and Young engaged in the first Test match against New Zealand at Lord's, found themselves short for their game against Somerset at Bath. Walter Robins and 'Gubby' Allen went out to the nets to have a look at the aspiring talent being coached by Fowler and Watkins, and collected Titmus.

So instead of selling scorecards at the Test, he was in the Middlesex side, aged sixteen years and six months. His career was subsequently interrupted by National Service in the Royal Air Force, but he got plenty of cricket for the RAF and Combined Services, and his first trip in an aeroplane piloted by Bob Wilson, now secretary of Nottinghamshire, was en route to play cricket for Combined Services.

The summer of 1955 saw Titmus, at the age of 22, establish himself among the leading all-rounders by recording his first 'double' in remarkable fashion. His total of wickets bounded to 191, average 16.31, and he nearly doubled his runs by scoring 1235, with a highest of 104. His tally of 158 wickets in all matches for Middlesex beat the previous county record set up by A. E. Trott, with 154, as far back as 1900.

Now he has done the 'double' eight times. He has taken more wickets for Middlesex than any other bowler; he did the hat-trick against Somerset at Weston-super-Mare in 1966, he took four wickets in six balls for England against New Zealand at Leeds in 1965, and in the same summer shared in a sixth-wicket record partnership for Middlesex of 227 with Clive Radley against the South Africans at Lord's. He has taken over 450 catches.

There is hardly room on his record card to mention that he also played soccer for Hendon and Watford, but it is as a cricketer of supreme qualities that he will long be remembered by the habitués of Lord's; when Titmus is gone, a piece of Lord's will be gone, but at the moment we are not thinking of the sunset of his illustrious career, but of new brave deeds he might perform this winter. We all wish him well.

*Fred Titmus was denied what might well have been a conspicuous opportunity to help win a Test against Australia when on the opening day of the Adelaide Test he was not brought on to partner Underwood as the Kent left-hander used a moist pitch to telling advantage. In four Tests of the 1974–75 series Titmus took only seven wickets at 51 apiece, yet his plucky 61 at Perth will be remembered.—Ed.*

# DOUG WALTERS

## by David Frith

*The Cricketer* January 1975

Kevin Douglas Walters had made hardly a run during the weeks leading up to the first Test, and was not *universally* expected to make the Australian XI. When he failed in the first innings of the Test his prospects dimmed further.

He has not, of course, appeared in Gallery in all its five years. Nor, more surprisingly, has he ever been one of *Wisden's* Five Cricketers of the Year – for the simple reason that his two tours of England have been disappointing, especially the last, in 1972, when he averaged less than eight in seven Test innings. He was dropped for the final Test, at The Oval, leaving Australia to field for the first time a side devoid of New South Wales players. Those excited claims, in 1965, that a batsman with the eye, timing and power of a Don Bradman had arrived had never seemed more absurd.

So much for the prosecution.

The defence, claiming that Walters is a world-class batsman who has merely had to endure, like all champions, occasional barren spells, might reach immediately for the evidence which many judges would consider flameproof (whisper it, for some walls have the ears of aesthetes) – figures! To the start of the series he had batted 80 times for Australia, making 3633 runs, with eleven centuries, average 50.46. That, at least, deserves a refrain.

Against England alone his figures were 1180 runs (three centuries) at 36.9; but to the start of the 1972 disaster they were 1126 at 45. Trumper, Ranji, Fry, Compton – all had series they would prefer to forget.

It is futile to pretend that he is at home on English pitches. In the coming summer, in his thirtieth year, he may yet be able to redress the balance in the four Tests in England. He has at least stated, with admirable fairness, that a good English pitch is better to bat on than a good

Doug Walters

Australian pitch. The ball comes off a little more slowly, giving a little extra time in which to adjust a stroke. This, to a man who regularly plays across the line, can be crucial.

Meanwhile, his great ability has been demonstrated at home, in India, in South Africa (moderately), in West Indies, and in New Zealand, where only last March he hit a staggering unbeaten 104 in less than three hours in a Test at Auckland. Fast left-arm bowler Collinge was too much for most of the Australians on a pitch, damp at one end, which yielded 18 wickets in the day.

A year earlier he averaged 71 against West Indies, his 112 at Port of Spain taking only 148 minutes and attracting all the superlatives. He made a hundred between lunch and tea on the first day, and this followed 102 not out in the previous Test and 55 and 108, both not out, against Trinidad.

So not all his stirring international deeds have been in the distant past.

His first Test match, just before his 20th birthday, was at Brisbane, against Mike Smith's England side. He made 155. He made another century in the second Test, at Melbourne, and averaged 68 for the series.

Two years later, as 2783873 Private Walters, K. D., he averaged 127 in two Tests against the touring Indians. He scored his 1000th Test run in only his 11th Test, on the 1968 tour of England. Later that year he scorched 699 runs (av. 116.5) off West Indies, climaxing the rubber with 242 and 103 at Sydney.

After this torrent of statistics, for which no forgiveness is asked, the defence might consider resting.

He was born – to parents who ran a dairy farm – on December 21, 1945, one day and many years after two other distinguished Australians, Sir Robert Menzies and Bill O'Reilly. All three were bush children – Walters from the Dungog area, not far from Maitland, which is C. G. Macartney country. Young Doug, guided unobtrusively by his father, and playing his cricket on the verandah and later on a pitch rolled out of antbeds, was a prodigious wicket-taker while in short pants, chalking up such outrageous figures as 9 for 8, 9 for 4, and 8 for 7 for the Police Boys

Club. Soon he developed a particular fascination for Anglo-Australian Test cricket – a fascination that is with him still.

What finally fired his ambition to play for Australia was sight of the 19-year-old Graeme Pollock blasting a century for South Africa at Sydney in 1963–64, although Walters himself was already ascending the magic ladder. In the previous season he was flown down to Sydney as a late replacement in the NSW Colts XI against Queensland. He came in at No. 7, a slight figure, incongruous large blue cap propped up by his ears, and scored 140 not out. One ball was pulled into the lake outside the Sydney No. 2 ground.

He was chosen for New South Wales, made 50 in his second innings (believing to this day that Wes Hall, for Queensland, refrained from bowling him a bouncer), and 60 in the next match. His first century in big cricket came the following year, pursued swiftly by another. He was on his way.

In 1964–65 he pulled out of a bad sequence by adding 378 for the second wicket at Adelaide with Lyn Marks – the second-highest of all partnerships in the 82-year history of the Sheffield Shield. Walters made 253 – and went on to take 7 for 63. Still he was only nineteen.

His Test career burst forth the next season, and he played in 35 Tests straight for which he was available (National Service keeping him from several, including a tour of South Africa) before being dropped at The Oval, 1972. Even in that personal dark hour his character showed through. Though his heart must have been sinking, he play-acted to the tour selectors in the interests of team spirits: 'Beauty! I won't have to be up early for nets!'

His wry humour has been recurringly useful to the side. He once broke the first-morning tension of a Test match, when there were several edgy newcomers in the dressing-room, by pushing his legs into his shirt-sleeves and trying to pull his flannels over his head, blurting out, Eric Sykes-style: 'Nervous? Who's nervous? Not me!'

That humour has been tested often enough . . . when he was given the State captaincy at 22 and allegedly asked two years later to issue a statement that it was too much for him and to give it up (he now leads the side once more) . . . when the hessian stand-covers went up in flames and a hundred bottles cascaded around him in the outfield at Bombay . . . when he was singled out by stone-throwing mobs in Calcutta who thought he had fought against Asians in Vietnam (his Army service had actually taken him only as far north as Queensland) . . . when he was caught for 74 off an apparent no-ball in a Test at Durban only to find that the umpire had stifled his call . . . when his inelegant efforts to play short-pitched balls from Procter and Pollock and Lever and Snow brought heaps of derision down upon him. And his humour has been tested in this season of 1974–75 up to the point where he came in on the fourth afternoon at Brisbane with all to lose. He hooked, and pulled to the sparsely-inhabited mid-wicket area, and drove handsomely, if with plenty of right shoulder, until Australia had advantage enough, and he had 62 welcome, welcome runs. If Australia are to regain the Ashes it seems likely that Doug Walters will have a good deal to do with the victory.

*Doug Walters certainly had much to do with Australia's victory in the second Test, at Perth, hitting a century between tea and close of play. On his third tour of England he again failed to dominate, though he happened to finish first in the tour averages with 784 runs at 60.31. His highest score in five Test innings was 65. He had always scored heavily off West Indies, but a severe knee injury, sustained when his spikes held as he twisted away from a bouncer in a Shield match, kept him out of the 1975–76 series. He turned 30 during the season, and there was speculation as to how much Test cricket was left in him.—Ed.*

# BISHAN BEDI

## by Tony Lewis

*The Cricketer* March 1975

When you have seen Bishan Singh Bedi twirl down his left-arm spinners after 60 overs with the same gentle rhythm and control as he first settled into at the start of his spell, you understand why his is a great bowling action. Even more so in his own country, where the test of stamina is more severe in burning heat and on hard-baked grounds which tug on the muscles and jar all the joints.

I have always thought that a great clockmaker would have been proud to have set Bedi in motion – a mechanism finely balanced, cogs rolling silently and hands sweeping in smooth arcs across the face. Yet it would be wrong to portray him as something less than human – all hardware and no heart – because he bowls with a fiery aggression which belies his gentle and genial nature. His rhythm too has only come after countless hours of practice in the nets.

His captains, who for most of his Test career have been 'Tiger' Pataudi and Ajit Wadekar, often introduced him to the attack within the first half hour of a Test innings. Indeed when England fell prey to the pressures of spin and close catching last time out in India, the brightly turbaned, left-arm spinner was seen loosening up at third man while Solkar was only in his second over.

That is not such crazy logic. On many overseas surfaces the shine is often gone within a quarter of an hour. So, without having genuine pace at their disposal, these Indian captains offered their high-class spinners a fairly new firm ball which settled easily into the hand and, most important of all, produced bounce at the batsman's end. Bedi thrived, with close fieldsmen leaping around the bat as batsmen attempted to fight through their first few overs.

Bishan Bedi was never formally taught the bowling skills. He confesses: 'As a young boy in Amritsar I just happened to get hold of a ball and roll it around as it left my hand.' So it is not surprising to learn that as the instinct to spin grew quickly, his stamina developed alongside, and the young man who had taken up the game only at the late age of thirteen at St Francis High School was making his début in first-class cricket two years later for Northern Punjab in the Ranji Trophy.

'I was lucky with my easy action,' he admits, inferring that it came naturally. 'It is smooth, I suppose, and I have spent hours developing the rhythm. So I am not like lots of other spinners who get sore fingers, you know, strains in the ankles and thighs. A good action spares you that. Do you know, I have never had finger trouble.'

The fine art of Bishan Bedi is based on his personal philosophy. He bowls to get wickets by deceiving batsmen, tricking them into false shots, crowding them initially, but carefully placing fielders to trap the one that looks like getting away. I once asked him if he bowled differently in attack than in defence. 'I have never bowled defensively,' he quickly came back at me. 'Some left-arm spinners in English cricket set their fields straight away, six on the off and three on the leg. I like a couple up close to start, especially with the new batsman – a slip, a gully and a square gully if I can, and then one on the leg side, because the batsman might fear the off trap and play outside the ball. I always bowl at the stumps. I have never bowled one side or the other just to contain.'

In an era when limited-overs cricket has pushed British spinners along the defensive road, blocking shots and waiting for the indiscriminate move by the batsman, Bedi's approach is becoming almost a treasure of the past. Or should we consider ourselves fortunate that the very best of the world's spinners like Bedi and Intikhab are playing in county cricket, and have flare-lit the way for young spinners and their coaches?

The skills he has acquired therefore are attacking skills. Apart from the orthodox spin which *leaves* the right-handed batsman, he also grips the ball less firmly and slides the wrist under it, genuinely under-cutting it, so that it goes straight on the other end, despite the appearance of

Bishan Bedi

genuine finger-spin. Another ball, seam up, with similar action, he floats down at rather quicker pace. It can dip into you through the air, though I must be honest, when I have faced him abroad, the ball that has intrigued me most is the seamer which appears to drift outwards towards the slips. It never seems to happen in England. Or is it just me? I must talk to Farokh Engineer and George Sharp, the men who keep wicket to him.

We return again to the personal qualities which have made Bedi exceptional even by the highest standards, because he is surely the best left-arm spinner in the world.

Running hopefully in pursuit of a ball along the boundary line he bounces along, one-paced, without ever being able to summon the muscle strength to slip his solidly-made body into third gear. His head rolls from side to side and a large smile tells the crowd that here is a man prepared to joke at his own limitations. They love him in India.

When the moment comes to bowl, the smile vanishes. A frown joins the pleats of the turban (patka, strictly speaking), a serious concentration. Classically, the eyes of aggression appear over the right shoulder, behind the raised right arm as he bowls. He beats the bat and he groans, does it twice and he hates. Yet should the victim leap from the crease and crack a six, the first applause will come from the bowler. Stoically Bishan Bedi casts his bait, over after over, each ball looking like the last, until the victim is drawn forward where the ball no more is, and that is the dream for which he endlessly toils for Northamptonshire and for India.

*Only two bowlers took more than Bishan Bedi's 85 wickets in the English season of 1975. Back in India, he was chosen to lead his country in the three matches against Sri Lanka, and then on the tour of New Zealand and West Indies. At the start of that tour he had taken 146 wickets in 39 Test matches.—Ed.*

# JEFF THOMSON

## by Ray Robinson

*The Cricketer* May 1975

Of all World Cup bowlers the one exciting most interest among cricket-watchers is Jeff Thomson, the human hurricane from Australia. Confronted by a bowler so swift, batsmen could think of safer games, such as Russian roulette.

As Thomsom walks to his mark to begin hostilities batsmen see a well-set-up man of 6ft 1in, scarcely looking 14 stone. A brown mane partly masks his shirt-collar. With the balance of a surfboard rider, his approach for most of his 15 running strides is as easy as a medium-pacer's– until the last three souped-up strides.

Near the line his right boot whips across behind the left for the take-off, slewing his broad shoulders side-on. From behind his right thigh a heave of arm propels the ball with a somewhat slinging action. In the explosive force of his high delivery his athletic body whirls around, pivoting on the ball of his left foot. Effort makes his blue eyes bulge like boiled lollies. Often his mouth opens roundly, a symbolic O.

In demeanour onlookers seldom see a trace of the hot-headed 17-year-old footballer suspended from soccer for having punched a rebuking referee. Though a magazine's quotes in 1974 set a startling high in callous bloodthirstiness (semi-jocular propaganda taken too literally, he implies) the 1975 Thomson mien scarcely fits specifications of savagery.

In fact, he is one of the quietest members of the Australian XI and is not one to stay yarning in the dressing room until the ice-box runs dry. Jeff doesn't wear his heart on his rolled sleeve – if he has a heart (some batsmen think a cobblestone has usurped its place).

217

Switches from end to end, rejected appeals, batsmen receiving roadside repairs, whatever a day brings he is unemotional on the field. One eminent writer, Keith Dunstan, looking for signs that he hates batsmen, described his manner as simply indifferent.

Jeffrey Robert Thomson was born in a Sydney suburb, Bankstown, an August 16, 1950. At 19 he preferred riding a board on Pacific surf to bowling eight-ball overs for Bankstown. He looked like being lost to cricket until his mate Len Pascoe persuaded him to resume at 20. Five matches for New South Wales at 22 lifted him into a Melbourne Test against Pakistan.

It was an erratic, wicketless anticlimax. Among his memories are that in the second innings his captain gave the new ball to medium-fast Max Walker instead. Thomson was refused a pain-killing injection for a lump in the ball of his left foot – swelling from a year-old part-mended crack in a bone. A doctor advised a winter's rest.

It was 13 months after that Test before NSW chose him again, all steamed up. His speed and bounce against Queensland drove wicketkeeper Brian Taber yards deeper than he had ever stood for any bowler – so far that he did well to hear 'No-ball!' called. Queenslanders lost the match but gained a bowler. They persuaded the resaddled terror to move to Brisbane, leaving his Sydney job as a concrete-pipe salesman.

In a Past v Present game for an infants' home Thomson took five balls to skittle former Test all-rounder Alan Davidson. Cajoled into speaking at a Town Hall reception afterwards, Davidson stepped forward, dropping a towel to the floor, and said: 'I throw in the towel, Jeff – you're too good for me.'

The frequency of Bob Willis's and Peter Lever's bumpers in the first innings of the Test series – especially Lever's three consecutive balls at the eighth man's chest –brought a predictable response from Lillee and Thomson, only much faster and steeper.

In a couple of overs Thomson can turn a thigh-pad into a Vienna schnitzel. His yorker jolts stumps to rare angles, looking as if paralytic drunk. Short-of-a-length balls

Jeff Thomson

endanger batsmen's gloves more than their bails. When he adds more venom to velocity a full-scale bouncer has wicketkeeper Rod Marsh leaping desperately to save four over-the-top byes.

In the Sydney Test Geoff Arnold greeted Lillee and Thomson, first ball, with bouncers that caused each to jerk his head back out of harm's way. When Arnold came in, a bouncer from Thomson, first ball, struck his arm. Extending his bowling arm toward Arnold, Jeff called inquiringly along the pitch: 'Square?'

For his 33 English wickets in 4½ Tests Australia's untrumped ace averaged a victim for every 44 balls (Lindwall's and Snow's Test striking rate was 60 balls). When I asked Jeff had he taken more wickets downwind than into the breeze he murmured: 'Wouldn't have a clue.' His quickest ball, 92mph, is swifter than Lillee's, yet judging between them is almost like picking a tigersnake from a copperhead.

For generations an illegal two-up school in Sydney has been known as Thommo's, so Thomson's nickname soon became 'Two-up'. As his only work during the Test series was on the field the bachelor board-rider lived on his cricket earnings, $1000 (approx. £600) in Test allowances plus a $1000 bonus voted from a lucrative series.

Five weeks after he strained the main tendon in his right shoulder at tennis in Adelaide a medical report considered him fit to bat and bowl in the season's last match but not to field in a position that could involve violent throwing. Thomson scored 61 (his highest) and took nine wickets, making 62 in 12 matches. Victorian captain Ian Redpath confessed: 'Jeff had us on the run.'

Above and below the Equator there is speculation about how much English wickets will allow of the speed and bounce produced in Australia. Besides England's batsmen, Sussex will be closely interested as Thomson has expressed a wish to make cricket his living.

*Once he had sorted out a no-ball problem Jeff Thomson became a force on England's slower pitches. His 5 for 38 put paid to England's second innings in the first Test and on the heartless Oval wicket he bowled with much life, taking five wickets in 52 overs. Failure in the first Test against West Indies proved nothing, since he remains a fast bowler who, on his day, is a match-winner and demoraliser of batsmen. He took four, five or six wickets in an innings in each of the last four Tests of the 1975–76 series, his ferocity repeatedly proving too much for the West Indians. Thomson crowned a successful season by landing a contract with a Brisbane radio station guaranteeing him £39,000 per annum for ten years, making him the world's most highly paid Test cricketer.—Ed.*

# ASIF IQBAL

## by Colin Cowdrey

*The Cricketer* June 1975

The Prudential World Cup this month will see Asif Iqbal as the captain of Pakistan for the first time. He celebrates his 32nd birthday on the day before it starts. If Intikhab's omission is a real surprise and the loss of his leg-spinning a disappointment for the crowds, at least no-one could quarrel with the new appointment. The cricket world has a special affection for Asif and Pakistan will inherit a host of new wellwishers.

Born in Hyderabad, he learnt his cricket in India, where he was regarded as a natural batsman who could be called upon to bowl. His father, Majeed Razui, a fine cricketer himself, died when Asif was six months old but happily several members of his family adored cricket and gave him every encouragement. He moved to Karachi when he was sixteen, a dramatic turn of events. Strangely, his new cricket mentors warmed to his bowling and rather under-estimated his ability with the bat. It is astonishing to watch Asif Iqbal today in full cry and to recall that he was selected for two major tours for Pakistan as an opening bowler.

His first-class career was launched in 1961 against Ted Dexter's MCC side. He took part in three unofficial Tests against the visiting Commonwealth XI, travelled also to Ceylon and East Africa, and with the Pakistan Eaglets toured England, taking a lot of wickets. In his first Test match, against Australia at Karachi, he took two wickets but it is significant that, batting No. 10, he scored 41 and 36. On his first major tour to Australia in 1965 he was the leading wicket-taker in the Test matches and headed the first-class bowling averages for the tour.

But those with good memories who were present at the first Test match in Wellington on January 26, 1965 will

222

Asif Iqbal

confirm it marked the emergence of a new batting star. New Zealand left Pakistan the task of scoring 259 to win but they soon found themselves 19 for 5 in the face of some magnificent fast bowling from Motz and Collinge. Asif, at No. 8, showed his mettle and followed his fine score of 30 in the first innings with a masterly and match-saving 52 not out.

Unaccountably, when Pakistan came to England in 1967 he was still looked upon as a bowler rather than a batsman. The bogey was finally laid in the Oval Test match when, with Pakistan 65 for 8 on the last day and about to be beaten by an innings and a lot of runs, Asif produced his soliloquy, 146 in three hours, the highest score by a No. 9 batsman in a Test match. England still won the match but Pakistan took the honours with Asif the man of the moment.

My first memory of him is watching him field under the tree at Canterbury, patrolling that vast boundary with more zest and speed than anyone I can remember. Leslie Ames and I, manager and captain of Kent respectively at that time, were captivated by his uncomplicated, joyous approach to cricket as well as his undoubted natural skills, and he joined Kent in 1968. After two comparatively lean years adjusting to English conditions everything seemed to come right in 1970. Kent could not have won the Championship that year without his glorious attacking batsmanship. Left 340 to win on the last day at Cheltenham, his innings of 109 against Allen, Mortimore and Bissex on a broken wicket, to win the match, was one of the highlights of his career. Who will forget the 91 that so nearly took Kent to victory against Lancashire in the Gillette Cup final of 1971 – and his long, sad walk back to the pavilion? Being Asif, he was bitterly disappointed, not because of the hundred he had missed but because he felt he had failed his team.

A back injury, sustained in 1964 at Sydney, keeps recurring if he bowls too much. With so much ability this has been a huge disappointment but, in truth, he has the fragile frame of the racehorse, not a workhorse, and in Kent we have now learnt to use him in short bursts. He has played an invaluable part as an occasional bowler in our one-day successes.

His colleagues feel that Asif the batsman lives too dangerously. If you are sitting with your pads on waiting to go in next you can feel very strongly about this at times. Despising all forms of defence he has a flair for attack. Unless all guns are firing he feels he is giving less than his best. W. G. Grace used to say, 'I hate defensive strokes – you can only score three off them.' This is Asif. However, this last year or two we have seen glimpses of a maturer, more measured approach. He is reluctant to concede it but he is beginning to see that even great players in top form balance attack with discretion. The responsibilities of his new position will bring more discipline. In consequence, I think we shall see Asif Iqbal emerge as a truly world-class player, his cavalier approach undiminished, giving more pleasure than ever before.

Most young cricketers would like to play like Asif. I would love to be as fleet of foot, throw caution to the winds and hit the ball with such gay abandon. What a thrill to run as fast between the wickets! He is a tough self-critic, a man of firm principles, fired with ambitions and high ideals which will be much in evidence long after his cricket days are over. He is now a Kentish Man, happily settled in Orpington with his wife Fahrana and two sons Omer and Hesham. It has intrigued me how a man of such soft heart and gentle nature can be such a master of destruction on the field. As a colleague he is generous and unselfish in the extreme and these characteristics will draw his men around him.

There are too many imponderables about captaincy to assess how well he will do. It can be such an easy game when everything goes to plan. Top-class sport is all about keeping calm under pressure.

I believe that Asif will succeed because over the years his best performances have been carved out when the odds are stacked against him. Moreover he has a warm heart and the knack of radiating fun. When he smiles it is spontaneous, it is infectious and everyone around is a little happier for his touch. An old-fashioned potion, maybe, but it is a priceless gift in a serious-minded, sometimes too competitive world.

*Pakistan were the unlucky side in the Prudential World Cup. They lost the vital West Indies match at Edgbaston when Murray and Roberts put on 64 for the tenth wicket to win the match and edge Pakistan out of the semi-finals. Asif Iqbal, absent after a minor operation, might have made a difference. Back in county cricket, he continued to be a great asset to Kent, heading their batting in 1975.—Ed.*

# JOHN MURRAY

## by Mike Brearley

*The Cricketer* July 1975

John Murray came on the MCC staff as a batsman in 1950, at the age of 15. He had learned the game at the Rugby Boys' Club, in Kensington. There were virtually no facilities at school, but the Boys' Club, for whom his father had also played, had a good ground and gave him the opportunity for competitive cricket, football, and boxing. JT was also, in those days, a footballer – he was offered terms by Brentford in 1952 – and a boxer – he was the boys' champion of Kensington.

He decided early to concentrate entirely on cricket. He also started to keep wicket. As often happens, the beginning was fortuitous; the regular 'keeper broke a finger during a game, and John stepped in. He had his debut for Middlesex in 1952. From 1953 to 1955 he played for a strong RAF side. He took over from Leslie Compton at the end of 1955, won his cap the next year, and for 20 years has been an automatic choice for Middlesex.

The rest of his career will be well known to readers of *The Cricketer*. He went on all the major tours except to West Indies, and to Australia twice. He played 21 times for England; I was surprised it was not more. In my memory he was as much *the* England wicketkeeper of the 1960s as Alan Knott is of the '70s. This summer he broke the world record for wicketkeeping dismissals.

One of the most striking features of JT's cricket is the stylishness of everything he does. He is completely relaxed, whether taking the ball, or stroking it wide of mid-on. His movements flow; when he is on form he makes it all look so easy. He himself stresses the importance of rhythm and tolerance. Of all his contemporaries as 'keepers he most admires Wally Grout. 'He was never on the ground except when actually diving for a catch.' John's own mannerisms, the tips of the gloves touched together, the peak of the cap touched, give him that feeling of relaxed rhythm that comes across so characteristically.

I asked him if he ever doubted his ability. Yes, he said, he did, right up to 1961 and his first series for England. He had had, after all, very little wicketkeeping experience by the time he became a regular county player. He never worried about standing back. I think he regards the real test to be one's ability standing up. We'd all agree, probably, but it's worth remembering how superlatively good JT was (he'd agree that a little of his agility is gone now) standing back.

It is impossible to talk of his career without talking also of Fred Titmus's. Fred is not easy to keep wicket to. For one thing, he bowls very straight; for another, he only really spins some of his deliveries; for a third, he has to be taken half the time at Lord's, where the bounce of the ball has always been uneven. The extent to which they have helped each other is incalculable; perhaps the debt Fred owes JT is slightly the greater, since he so often can 'feel' what sort of pace Fred should bowl at, what line, and so on.

My clearest image of John's keeping is of the way he catches the ball. There could be no better model – fingers down, hands relaxed, and a long easy 'give' to one side or other of the body.

His batting has, overall, disappointed many. He agrees that he has never concentrated on it and worked at it as he would have done if it had not been his second string. And it is unlikely that anyone could be both a front-line batsman and a wicketkeeper over a long period in county cricket without losing something of his zest for and concentration in the latter job. At his best, he's a wonderful batsman. He often is at his best against fast bowling (he's a fine hooker and driver) and against slow bowling (he uses his feet and hits beautifully over the top). I think that it is characteristic of him that he should be least 'turned on' when playing against medium-pacers, where perhaps grafting would pay.

He is also a man for an occasion, an entertainer. He often saves his best performances for Yorkshire or Surrey, and is less likely to sparkle on a damp day at Ashby-de-la-Zouch.

I asked John about his disappointments in cricket. He has, after all, achieved almost all that an ambitious young

John Murray

man could have hoped for. The one disappointment that he mentioned was that Middlesex have never yet won anything during his career. He thinks the best sides he played for were those of the late '50s and early '60s, though he admits that one tends to bring together in memory people who didn't in fact overlap. We have always, however, lacked one or two top-class bowlers to support Titmus and, at different times, Warr, Moss and Price.

Standards of cricket have declined overall, John believes. He is inclined to connect this with the gradual lessening of discipline in cricket and outside. I think that by 'discipline' he sometimes means hardship and knowing one's place. When he came on the MCC staff his place was clear, and very low in the hierarchy. Lord's was then, he says, a way of life. He never resented the fact that he had to sweep the stands, that he had only one session a week reserved for net practice (they had to find time outside working hours for the rest of their practice), or that he was not allowed in the pavilion unless he was actually playing in the game. But the ambition was clearer and stronger; he could see exactly what he wanted to achieve, and what he wanted to get away from. Today, he thinks, it is perhaps too easy for young cricketers, and too many of them think they know too much. And of course you do need discipline to play this game well.

He also believes in enjoying his cricket. At a lunch earlier this season, JT said to the younger Middlesex players 'Play properly and enjoy yourselves'. He has done both for 25 years. First-class cricket will have lost a landmark when he retires at the end of this season.

*One of the memorable moments of the 1975 season was John Murray's final walk to the crease at Lord's – in the Benson & Hedges Cup final against Leicestershire. He was cheered by a standing audience all the way, and he acknowledged the reception with all the grace and poise long associated with him. He retired as the wicketkeeper with most dismissals and most catches in the history of first-class cricket, and was made MBE in the 1976 New Year's Honours.—Ed.*

# ALVIN
# KALLICHARRAN

## by Tony Cozier

*The Cricketer* August 1975

The biographical minutae which appear next to the names of players in the cricket annuals and yearbooks generally reveal very little. In the case of Kallicharran, Alvin Isaac (b Port Mourant, Berbice, B G. 21 Mar 49. LHB occ LB) they happen to be more than just a notation of where and when one of the most proficient of contemporary batsmen was born. There is a significance about both the place and the time.

Port Mourant is a small town in Berbice county along Guyana's east coast. Its inhabitants are almost totally employed in the sugar industry, which dominates much of the country's rural life. In the 1950s it became a phenomenal nursery for Guyanese and West Indian cricket as, simultaneously, three players of extraordinary ability emerged from its previously unknown precincts to gain international acclaim.

Young Kallicharran grew up in a community basking in the reflected glory of its famous cricketing sons – Rohan Kanhai, Basil Butcher and Joe Solomon. He needed no encouragement to take to a game which was the main topic of male conversation after a hard day in the canefields. Although small and frail in build, he obviously possessed excellent eyesight and keen ball sense. All the ingredients were there for the making of another Port Mourant Test player.

The outstanding success of Kanhai, Butcher and Solomon was the catalyst for another development beneficial to those who followed in their wake. Previously, cricket in British Guiana (as it was before becoming independent in 1966) had been concentrated almost entirely in Georgetown, the capital. Those outside took part in an annual lottery to see which of them would fill the four places allotted to the country districts in the annual trials for selection on the British Guiana team. The story is told of how Kanhai only qualified at first because of illness to someone else. It was a system which had to change once it became clear what potential lay even in an area as small as Port Mourant.

So Kallicharran and others of his era needed no luck to win recognition – only ability, and of this there was no scarcity.

Solomon once told me he was never in any doubt that Kallicharran would one day be a great player.

His progress has been predictable and uninterrupted – through the Guyana Schools team in the West Indies championships in 1966, into the Guyana Shell Shield team the following year, into the Test team in 1972 (in the most spectacular fashion with successive centuries against New Zealand) and into county cricket with Warwickshire in 1972. In the selection of any World XI, it is difficult to see how he could be omitted at present.

In his 22 Tests, Kallicharran has repeatedly demonstrated that he is the complete batsman – as comfortable in a crisis as in a dominant situation; as facile against pace as against spin; as ideally equipped to take advantage of a perfect pitch as he is to battle on an impaired one.

If his thrilling exhibition against Australia in the first-round Prudential Cup match at The Oval exemplified his most ebullient mood and his ability to cope with true pace, it must be said that conditions were ideal and the match was of the limited-overs variety by which the purists refuse to measure standards.

In 1973, in the enthralling third Test against Australia, at Port-of-Spain, when West Indies were set 334 to win on a spinner's pitch, the diminutive left-hander played an astonishing innings of 91 which almost brought his team victory. There were at least half a dozen catches in the short-leg region in that match yet, every time Kallicharran played forward, he dropped the ball dead at his feet and never gave the semblance of a chance.

A year later, at the same venue, in conditions now

Alvin Kallicharran

favouring the faster bowlers, England collapsed for 131 and West Indies were 147 for 5 midway through the second day. By the end of play (made infamous by his 'run out' by Greig) Kallicharran was 142 out of 274 for 7 – and the next-highest individual score had been Sobers's 23.

The one innings which he will cherish above all others, however, must be his 124 at Bangalore in the first Test against India last year. Rain and late and inadequate covering produced the most treacherous Test pitch I have ever seen and, by his own admission, the most difficult Kallicharran has ever played on. The ball turned viciously and stopped. Venkataraghavan would repeatedly pitch outside the left-hander's leg stump – and be collected by Engineer in front of first slip. From an overnight 212 for 2, West Indies were all out for 289. Of the 77 added, Kallicharran scored 64 without playing one false shot until he was last out for 124 caught behind off a ball which turned a mile. It had been the innings of a master batsman.

Kallicharran's claims to being a player for all climes and conditions is reflected in his record – 1827 Test runs at an average of 57.09 with a century against all opponents except Australia (highest score 91). He has repeatedly proved his worth for Warwickshire where not the least of his virtues has been his obvious enjoyment of the game. While most of his West Indian team-mates were, naturally, complaining about having to rejoin their counties for a John Player League match the day after the nerve-racking World Cup Final, Kallicharran not only was eager to play – he also made 72.

Like everyone else, Kallicharran has his weaknesses, even though they may be fewer than most. One appears to be a lack of stamina needed to endure a long series. Against Australia in 1973 and England in 1973 and 1974 he started in magnificent form only to fade into low scores towards the end. After his long innings against Australia at Port-of-Spain in 1973, nervous exhaustion led to his being confined to bed for two days.

Generally, Kallicharran has been compared to Kanhai. There can be little doubt that he has modelled himself on his illustrious countryman and that he is very much the left-handed version. Similar in height, build and looks, even his stance at the wicket is a mirror-image. Nevertheless, it was interesting to hear an Australian seeing him for the first time, R. S. Whitington, state that he revived memories of Neil Harvey.

Only 26, Alvin Kallicharran is merely at the start of what must surely be a great cricketing career. Married with a son not quite two, he is a wholehearted, dedicated cricketer who neither smokes nor drinks. He loves the game and, far from going stale, his edge seems to be sharpened by a surfeit of it.

*In his 23rd Test, the first of the 1975–76 series in Australia, Alvin Kallicharran scored his seventh Test century. In the next, at Perth, he was struck in the face and his nose was broken. His modesty and his philosophy should carry him through his ups and downs. Former West Indies fast bowler Wes Hall believes that 'Kalli' could eventually pass Sir Garfield Sobers's record Test aggregate.—Ed.*

# RODNEY MARSH

## by Ray Robinson

*The Cricketer* September 1975

In a long-suffering race – wicketkeepers – Rodney Marsh is the one whose activities have most in common with a railway-siding buffer and a box-kite. At the receiving end of Australia's high-speed battery, the solid West Australian has the tough physique and resilient spirit to stand up to bruising pressures without giving ground.

Since Jeff Thomson joined Dennis Lillee in using a new ball as a projectile, Marsh has the most stressful job of any international 'keeper I have seen. The range he has to cover is the widest. His leaps for bouncers are the highest, bordering on ethereal. His sprints up to the stumps to receive fieldsmen's returns are the longest. On the fastest wickets the bowlers' velocity has driven him up to 27 paces behind the sticks – further than Godfrey Evans stood for Frank Tyson in Australia.

Errant balls streaking down the leg side make normal footwork inadequate. Before you can say Jeff Thomson, Rod launches himself at them with a horizontal heave. Nature has considerably cushioned his hips for landings.

Amid a busy sequence of matches in Australia last season Marsh's pummelled hands had to be rested from his State's match against MCC. Sometimes he tucked them under his armpits, much like a caned schoolboy trying to ease smarting palms. Watching Rod wind tape around each finger and pack his gloves with foam rubber, Greg Chappell asked, 'What's the date of your bout with Tony Mundine, Bacchus?'

This nickname is no hangover from days when Marsh was plump enough to have personified the Roman god of wine. When an interstate train stopped at a Victorian country station players saw the name MARSH in large letters. As the train moved they read its full name BACCHUS MARSH.

Rodney Marsh

Born on November 4, 1947, Rodney William Marsh is five years younger than his tall brother Graham, whose golf earnings around the world dwarf the modest rewards international cricket yields. So that he could keep wicket for the WA University XI Rod entered an arts course.

While a third-year student he scored 0 and 104 on his début for WA against West Indies at 20, standing on the left-hand side of the bat. He is a right-hander in everything else.

To shed lard-like layers from a 15½-stone figure 5ft 8½ins tall, Marsh said, 'I gave up my favourite drink, beer, each winter, cut out potatoes and bread and trimmed lunch to three pieces of fruit.' Greater love hath no man than that he lay down his knife (and fork) to ascend in his chosen sport.

Choice of Marsh, 23, as Test 'keeper, replacing popular Brian Taber, 30, caused groans in Sydney, gasps in Brisbane (home city of John Maclean, 24) and glee in Perth. I assumed that selectors Sir Donald Bradman, Neil Harvey and Sam Loxton felt there was so little between leading 'keepers that they chose the one with most batting potential.

Australia's youngest-ever 'keeper had kept in only 13 first-class games. Test-début nervousness was heightened by his having felt almost a stranger in the team room. 'Except for Garth McKenzie, I hardly knew a soul,' he said, 'though I'd played against some of them once or twice.'

Rod held four catches in his first Test but three chances of sorts escaped from his podgy paws. Through John Snow's golf chum Guy Wolstenholme word came that the English XI had nicknamed Marsh 'Irongloves'. Guy and Peter Thomson ribbed Graham about his younger brother, for whom most critics could not find a good word. Rod's self-criticism was almost as harsh; feeling unworthy of the green cap, he left it in his locker and finished the Brisbane Test bareheaded.

'I felt worse for being shown up by Alan Knott, keeping like a dream,' he recalls. Knott was credited with the finest season ever by a visiting wicketkeeper – a star who made the semi-streamlined West Australian seem like a bit player.

A big heart and an unquenchable sense of humour brought Rod through without his nerve cracking. Recovery of confidence was symbolised by the green cap reappearing to shade his brown eyes.

Before he turned 25 Marsh rose to be a topliner. Lillee gratefully acknowledged his agile support. While England's batsmen could not pick Massie's either-way swing, Rod knew which way each ball would veer. His 23 wickets in five Tests in 1972 set a record for a series in England.

He had been 92 in a Melbourne Test when the innings was declared before he could make himself the first 'keeper to score 100 for Australia. One of Rod's philosophic comments: 'I might have got out at 99.'

In a hopeless situation at Old Trafford on his first visit the outplayed Australians were losing dismally. Marsh lifted their spirits with a valiant 91; four sixes sailed into the crowd in a few overs. Since that buccaneering onslaught the sight of Rod taking guard tends to give bowlers feelings like those of ancient mariners seeing a ship run the Jolly Roger to the masthead.

Two of his seven centuries before the present tour were in Tests – 132 against New Zealand and 118 against Pakistan. His thunderous 236 for WA against the Pakistanis is the highest score by an Australian wicketkeeper in 93 years since Murdoch's 321 for NSW.

Stuart Surridge ranks Marsh 'the greatest keeper to pace bowling the world has seen.' As Surrey skipper, Surridge saw Don Tallon taking Lindwall and Miller.

I have come across nothing to rival such a roundly-criticised cricketer's rapid rise to dynamic influence in a Test side. In discernment of potential it ranks as a selection masterpiece.

Untidily effective, Marsh has more important things to do than tuck his shirt in. By day's end his flannels often bear green and brown stains. His conversation has down-to-earth touches, too. Originally a high school teacher, he is now a Swan Brewery market development executive, with a 3½-year-old son.

No 'keeper had reached 50 wickets in an Australian summer until his 64 in 14 matches last season. Asked about his best catch, he reflected: 'Getting one glove to a far-out leg-side chance from Bevan Congdon off Tangles Walker in the 1974 Auckland Test.' It was Marsh's 100th wicket in 25 Tests. Only Wally Grout reached that figure in fewer Tests (24). Knott's 100th came in his 30th Test. Deryck Murray has 87 in 29 Tests for West Indies, Ken Wadsworth 85 in 30 for New Zealand and Farokh Engineer 82 in 42 Tests for India.

Marsh is at the heart, as well as the hub, of the outcricket that has lifted Australia from the depths of 1971 to the heights of 1975. He means so much to the Australian XI that if he missed a Test through injury or illness, dismay would be felt across 3000 miles from Perth to Surfers Paradise.

*Rod Marsh is quite as important to Australia's fortunes and plans as Knott is to England's. With 55 Tests behind him – in which he had made 134 dismissals and 1731 runs at the impressive average of 35.32 – to the end of the 1975 series against England, his skill and his unquenchable aggression should continue to keep Australia among the most successful sides in modern Test history. In the 1975–76 series against West Indies his 26 dismissals equalled John Waite's world Test record. Captain of Western Australia, Marsh is tipped to succeed Ian Redpath as Australia's vice-captain.—Ed.*

# MUSHTAQ MOHAMMAD

## by John Arlott

*The Cricketer* October 1975

Mushtaq Mohammad is recognised as an outstanding cricketer, but not always for all the valid reasons. His public image is not completely exact. He is remembered as 'the youngest' – the youngest man to play first-class cricket (at 13 and 41 days); to appear in a Test (at 15 years 124 days); and to score a Test century (at 17 years 82 days). When he made his first major tour of England, in 1962, he was a lad of 18, but he did enough to become one of *Wisden's* Cricketers of the Year. His chubby cheeks, 'cherubic' expression, white smile and modest manner emphasized the impression of youth. He could be a buoyantly attacking batsman and often would switch the bat in his hands to play a ball from a left-arm spinner, in effect, left-handed. So an idea was fostered that Mushtaq was a gay, boyish, carefree cricketer. In truth he is as stern a competitor as any of his competitive brothers – or as any cricketer in the world. That first Test century at Delhi in 1960–61 was played to save a Test and the rubber against India; his second, against England at Trent Bridge in 1962, lasted over five hours and drew the match.

He is, by nature and urge, a strokemaker, especially against pace bowling, which he hooks and cuts brilliantly and, at opportunity, will drive wristily. Yet, in many ways, he has inherited from his brother Hanif as the anchorman of the Pakistan batting. He too is deeply conscious of his family's reputation. In 1962, when Hanif was troubled by a knee injury, Mushtaq, at 18, scored more runs than any other member of the team both in Tests and on the entire tour of England. In Pakistan's entire history as a Test-playing country they have never taken the field without one of the sons of Ismail Mohammad and Amir Bee.

241

Born at Jumagadh in India, but brought to Pakistan at the time of Partition, all five of the brothers who grew to manhood – in order of age, Wazir, Raees, Hanif, Mushtaq and Sadiq – played first-class cricket; once all in the same match. All were Test players for Pakistan except Raees, whom his mother thought the most brilliant of the five and who was once told he would play against India, only to be made twelfth man.

Mushtaq is superbly technically equipped with a sharp eye, instinctive identification of length, nimble footwork, an innate sense of timing and the striking power of a compactly-built and muscular 13 stone man. He is a fine, and frequently brilliant, batsman against any bowling. Under all his skills lies the determination, the concentration and the reluctance to get out which mark the good professional.

All this might suggest Mushtaq is a batsman pure and simple. On the contrary, there is barely a better leg-spinner in the world. He is more accurate than most of that kind, genuinely spins the ball, and hides his googly well. Only two current wrist -spinners, Chandrasekhar and Intikhab, have taken more than his 40 wickets in Tests. His ability is such that often one wonders whether, if he were not a good batsman, he might not be substantially effective solely as a leg-spinner.

While he has scored over 25,000 runs at an average of about 42, he has taken nearly 800 wickets at 23. When he first came to England – with the Pakistani Eaglets of 1958 at the age of 14 – he kept wicket. Since then he has been a nimble fieldsman in the covers and a safe catcher close to the bat.

Mushtaq was already a mature cricketer at first-class and Test level when he joined Northamptonshire in 1964 at the age of 20. While he was qualifying for Championship play he won the 1965 single-wicket tournament at Lord's. He has made two centuries in a match – and quite beguiling they were – and won a Gillette Man of the Match award. Now, still only 31, he has played in 36 Tests, more than any other current Pakistani except the – sadly – deposed Intikhab. His Test batting average is 42.27, exceeded only

Mushtaq Mohammad

among contemporary Pakistani players – by a mere .19 – by his younger brother, Sadiq.

Once the impression of Mushtaq as a light-hearted cricketer is dispelled, he becomes one to be savoured. Before he faces any ball he gives his bat the Mohammad family twirl and then, stern jutting, he is prepared to face whatever the bowler may deliver.

Whether he attacks or defends, he is an entertaining batsman to watch because he is so fluid in movement, so balanced, adroit and essentially aggressive. His resistance is never graceless nor lacking in imagination. In the most dogged innings he will identify the punishable ball and demolish it with a splendid punitive stroke.

Northamptonshire hired wisely when they engaged Mushtaq. Next year he has a benefit; from which, if his county's cricket-followers are just, he should do well. Yet, at 31 he still has at least ten years of effective cricket in him. Indeed, it may be that we have yet to see the best of him.

*Still only 32, Mushtaq Mohammad, if he maintains form, should attain very impressive figures by the time his playing days are over. Above all, his style and approach are an adornment to the game. He was appointed as Northamptonshire's captain in 1976.—Ed.*

# DENNIS LILLEE

## by David Frith

*The Cricketer* March 1976

There have been faster bowlers than Dennis Lillee, but not many. There have been more hostile fast bowlers, but not many. Spofforth, Ernie Jones, Constantine, Heine, Charlie Griffith, Andy Roberts, Jeff Thomson – all have brought menace, even terror, to the bowling crease. Lillee concedes nothing to any of them.

He is one of the great fast bowlers of the twentieth century, possessing a full set of gear changes, a knowledge of aerodynamics equal to Lindwall's, an abundance of stamina and determination, and more courage than is given to most.

He needed that courage in 1973 and '74 when he set about achieving one of sport's most impressive comebacks. The four stress fractures in the lower vertebrae would have finished many a career. Lillee, having dramatically bowled his way to fame, was faced with six weeks in plaster and a long and gruelling fight to full fitness. He withstood the punishment and handsomely repaid those who had worked with him and believed in him. He played cricket again, though only as a batsman. Then he put himself on to bowl. No twinges. At the end of the 1973–74 season his hopes were at least as high as the highest of his notorious bouncers.

England arrived next season to defend the Ashes in six Test matches. Lillee pronounced himself fit and dismissed Ian Chappell two or three times in early-season interstate fixtures. Australia selected him again. And in the first Test a new extermination firm was formed: Lillee and Thomson. England's batsmen at Brisbane would just as happily have taken their chances in the company of Leopold and Loeb, or Browne and Kennedy, or, at the end of the day, Burke and Hare. It was devastating, still fresh in memory.

Australia's opening pair took 58 wickets in the series out

of 108 that fell to bowlers – this despite Thomson's with-drawal through injury halfway through the fifth Test and Lillee's after six overs in the final match with a damaged foot.

The full force of this controlled cyclone was felt in the 1975 series, though England's sleeping pitches absorbed some of the energy. This was when Lillee's other bowling skills asserted themselves. As in the 1972 series, when he took a record 31 Test wickets, Lillee beat batsmen by change of pace and with his wicked awayswinger. Rod Marsh and the ever-expectant slips cordon did the rest. He had more support now: from the tireless Walker, from Gilmour (who would have strolled into any other Test team in the world), and from Thomson whenever he had his rhythm.

This winter, interrupted only by pleurisy, he has gone on to torment and punish the West Indians, taking his hundredth Test wicket in the process. Still that remade and wonderfully broad back held up against the pounding constantly dealt it by its owner.

Dennis Lillee's inspiration, when only a boy, came from a West Indian: Wes Hall, the genial fast-bowling giant. The young fellow from Perth, born on W. G. Grace's 101st birthday (July 18, 1949), clambered with all the fervour of a Beatles fan into the members' enclosure at the WACA ground just to be near his idol. There was also Graham McKenzie, the pride of Perth, to fan the flames of his ambition. And Fred Trueman. And Alan Davidson.

Not that this was enough. There had to be an inherent talent. The tearaway with long sideburns, who stormed in over a long distance and hurled his wiry body into delivery with every ounce of his might, eventually played for West-ern Australia. By 1970–71 he was considered good enough to play for Australia – one of the hopes in a reshaping of the national eleven. He took 5 for 84 against England at Adelaide in his maiden Test, opening the attack with another young aspirant, Thomson – Alan ('Froggy'), not Jeff.

A season in Lancashire League cricket with Haslingden followed. Next he bowled against a conglomerate team

Dennis Lillee

billed as the Rest of the World. In Perth he decimated them with 8 for 29, including 6 for 0 in one red-hot spell (when he wasn't feeling too well!): Gavaskar, Engineer, Clive Lloyd, Greig and Sobers were among the victims. The wider world at last took notice and wanted to know all about him.

He was learning all the time, especially when trying to bowl to Sobers during his indescribably brilliant 254 at Melbourne, when straight-drives came bouncing back from the boundary before the bowler had raised himself upright in the followthrough. Yet he continued to harass the tourists, not by any means now trying to bowl every ball at top speed, and if England in the spring of 1972 thought Australian claims of Lillee's bounce and penetration were exaggerated, the threat was soon a vivid reality.

He has sometimes attacked batsmen with his tongue – and been denounced for it. Brian Statham used to let the ball do all his talking. Fred Trueman's ripe language was somehow not the antithesis of geniality. Dennis Lillee's 'verbal aggression' has been something else in its spirit of near-hatred. One could name others in cricket history who have gone about their business in this way, only to be left with the feeling that in each case the bowler has failed in one respect to do himself justice. Lillee was a central figure in Australia's re-emergence as a formidable side, and a great deal has continued to be expected of him. The chanting of the crowds, the persistent publicity, the inescapable typecasting, the need to transpose celebrity into a real-world security – all this must take a man away from himself, at least in part.

A truth that will remain is that Perth has given to cricket a fast bowler, of hawklike countenance and perfect physique for his purpose, whose flowing approach and superb athletic action have been a thrilling spectacle for young and old, male and female, pacifist and warrior.

# WHO'S WHO OF
# CONTRIBUTORS

Arthur Reginald (REX) ALSTON b. July 2, 1901, Faringdon, Berks. Educated Trent College and Clare, Cambridge. All-round sportsman, excelling at athletics. Captained Bedfordshire in Minor County cricket in 1932 and played much good club cricket. Schoolmaster for many years. BBC staff 1942–61, broadcasting on Test and county cricket, rugby, tennis, athletics etc. Author of *Taking the Air* (1951), *Over to Rex Alston* (1953), *Test Commentary* (1956), *Watching Cricket* (1962). Regular contributor to *Playfair Cricket Monthly* and *The Cricketer*, and sportswriter for the *Daily Telegraph*.
GALLERY SUBJECT: Geoff Arnold.

Leslie Thomas JOHN ARLOTT, OBE b. February 25, 1914, Basingstoke, Hants. Educated Queen Mary's School, Basingstoke. Southampton police officer 1934–45; BBC talks and poetry producer 1945. Club cricketer in Hampshire as off-spinner with 'questionable' action and 'dull' batsman. Has given commentary on Test cricket since 1946 and has written extensively on the game, latterly for *The Guardian*. Honorary MA from Southampton University. Other major interests: wine, cheeses, topography. Stood twice as Liberal candidate in general elections. Over thirty books on cricket, including *Gone to the Test Match* (1948), *From Hambledon to Lord's* (1948), *Concerning Cricket* (1949), *Vintage Summer: 1947* (1967), *The Noblest Game* (with Sir Neville Cardus) (1969), *Fred* (1971), several tour books, and *The Oxford Companion to Sports and Games* (edited 1975).
GALLERY SUBJECTS: Alan Knott, Peter Lever, Tony Lewis, Mushtaq Mohammad, Garfield Sobers.

TREVOR Edward BAILEY b. December 3, 1923, Westcliff, Essex. Educated Dulwich and Cambridge (cricket and football Blues). Fast-medium bowler, dour right-hand batsman, fine fieldsman. Essex debut 1946; secretary

from 1954; captain 1961. All-rounder for England in 61 Tests 1949–59: 2290 runs, 132 wickets. Highest score 205 Essex *v* Sussex, Eastbourne, 1947. Best bowling 10 for 90 *v* Lancashire, Clacton, 1949. Sports correspondent to *The Financial Times* (earlier with *The Observer*). BBC 'comments man' during Test broadcasts. Books include *Playing to Win* (1954), *Championship Cricket* (1961), *The Best of My Time* (1968); editor of *John Player Cricket Yearbook*. In preparation, a biography of Sir Garfield Sobers.
GALLERY SUBJECTS: John Edrich, Ray Illingworth, Rohan Kanhai.

Richard (RICHIE) BENAUD, OBE b. October 6, 1930, Penrith, New South Wales, Australia. Educated Parramatta High School. Debut NSW 1948–49; for Australia 1951–52. 63 Tests: 248 wickets (record for Australia) with leg-spinners/googlies; 2201 runs at 24.45, including three centuries (one in 78 minutes *v* West Indies). Captain in 28 Tests. Record 266 wickets for NSW in 73 Sheffield Shield matches. Fine gully fieldsman. All-year-round cricket correspondent and television commentator. Books include *Way of Cricket* (1961), *A Tale of Two Tests* (1962), *The New Champions* (1965), *Willow Patterns* (1969).
GALLERY SUBJECTS: Bob Massie, Keith Stackpole.

John Michael (MIKE) BREARLEY b. April 28, 1942, Harrow, Middlesex. Educated City of London School and Cambridge (captain 1963–64; record aggregate of 4310 runs for the University). Debut Middlesex 1961; appointed captain 1971. Highest score 312 not out MCC Under-25 *v* North Zone, Peshawar, 1966–67. Left the game in late 1960s to do post-graduate studies in philosophy and to lecture in USA. Led Middlesex to two Lord's cup finals in 1975 – both matches lost. Has written perceptively about cricket in newspapers and *The Cricketer*.
GALLERY SUBJECT: John Murray.

Richard Trevor (DICK) BRITTENDEN b. August 22, 1919, Rakaia, Canterbury, New Zealand. Sports editor of

*The Press,* Christchurch since 1955. Author of five books, including *Great Days in New Zealand Cricket* (1958) and *New Zealand Cricketers* (1961). Twice won New Zealand journalism awards. Covered cricket tours of England, South Africa, India and Pakistan. Navigator in RNZAF during War, serving in UK and Bahamas. New Zealand correspondent to *The Cricketer.*
GALLERY SUBJECT: Bevan Congdon.

Michael COLIN COWDREY, CBE b. December 24, 1932, Bangalore, India. Educated Tonbridge and Oxford (captain 1954). Debut Kent 1950, capped 1951 (youngest for county at 18). Captain 1957–71, leading them to County Championship 1970. Only player to appear in 100 Tests (114): 7624 runs, 22 centuries, 120 catches. Led England 27 times. Retired from full-time cricket after 1975 season: 42,661 runs, highest score 307 MCC *v* South Australia, Adelaide, 1962–63. 100th century, Maidstone, 1973. A director of *The Cricketer,* to which he has been a regular contributor for some years. Wrote *Cricket Today* (1961), *Time for Reflection* (1962) and an autobiography, 1976.
GALLERY SUBJECTS: Asif Iqbal, Bernard Julien.

Winston Anthony Lloyd (TONY) COZIER b. July 10, 1940, Bridgetown, Barbados. Educated Lodge School, Barbados and Carleton University, Ottawa. Sports editor *Barbados Daily News* 1960–68. Has covered every Test in Caribbean since 1962 for newspapers and radio and toured with most recent West Indies teams. Editor of *West Indies Cricket Annual* since inception 1970. Played top-class club cricket for Carlton and Wanderers in Barbados. West Indies correspondent to *The Cricketer.*
GALLERY SUBJECT: Alvin Kallicharran.

GERARD Edward DENT b. July 19, 1928, Chelsea, London. Contributed cricket and football reports to *The Observer* 1968–72; also book reviews and features. 'Part-time amateur' playwright. Cricket addict with only 'very modest attainments' on field of play.
GALLERY SUBJECT: Graham McKenzie.

Edward PATRICK EAGAR b. March 9, 1944, Cheltenham, Gloucs. Educated Cheltenham and Cambridge. Cricket's best-known photographer. Took cameras to South Africa 1964 and Vietnam 1966. Covered MCC tours of West Indies 1973–74 and Australia 1974–75, Australian tour of West Indies 1973, West Indies tour of Australia 1975–76. Awarded Press Photographs of the Year prize for colour feature section 1973. Special photographer to *The Cricketer* since 1970.

DAVID Edward John FRITH b. March 16, 1937, Paddington, London. Educated Canterbury High School, Sydney, Australia. First-grade cricket for Paddington club, Sydney. Has written for many British and overseas newspapers. Appointed Editor of *The Cricketer* February 1973. Books: *Runs in the Family* (with John Edrich) (1969), '*My Dear Victorious Stod*' (1970) (Cricket Society Jubilee Literary Award), *The Archie Jackson Story* (1974), *The Fast Men* (1975), contributions to *The Oxford Companion to Sports and Games* (1975) and *Cricket: More than a Game*. GALLERY SUBJECTS: Greg Chappell, Doug Walters, Dennis Lillee.

ALAN GIBSON b. May 28, 1923, Sheffield, Yorks. Educated Farmer Road School, Leyton, Taunton School and Oxford. President of Oxford Union. First BBC cricket commentary given 1948; first Test broadcast 1962. Regular broadcaster on variety of topics in West Country. Cricket and rugby correspondent to *The Times*. Books: *Jackson's Year* (1965), *Game for Anything* (1973) (with David Foot and Derek Robinson), *A Mingled Yarn* (1976). GALLERY SUBJECTS: Tony Greig, Mike Procter.

James Maurice (JIM) KILBURN b. July 8, 1909, Sheffield, Yorks. Educated Holgate Grammar School and Sheffield University. Played in Yorkshire Council and Bradford League. *Yorkshire Post* cricket correspondent for 40 years until retirement. Books include: *In Search of Cricket* (1937), *History of Yorkshire County Cricket 1924–49* (1950), *Cricket Decade* (1959), *Thanks to Cricket*

(1972) (Cricket Society Jubilee Literary Award), *Over-throws* (1975).
GALLERY SUBJECTS: Brian Close, Tom Graveney.

James Charles (JIM) LAKER b. February 9, 1922, Brad-ford, Yorks. Educated Saltaire High School. War service with RAOC in Middle East. Debut Surrey 1946. One of the greatest off-spin bowlers the game has known. Took 19 for 90 in Old Trafford Test *v* Australia, 1956; 8 for 2 in 1950 Test trial at Bradford. In 46 Tests took 193 wickets at 21.23; 46 in 1956 series (second to S. F. Barnes's record 49). Toured Australia, West Indies, South Africa with MCC. 1944 wickets in career. Books: *Spinning Round the World* (1957), *Over to Me* (1960). BBC television commentator.
GALLERY SUBJECT: Intikhab Alam.

Anthony Robert (TONY) LEWIS b. July 6, 1938, Swansea, Glamorgan. Educated Neath Grammar School and Cambridge (captain 1962). Debut Glamorgan 1955; captain 1967–72. Retired end of 1974 season after recur-ring knee injury. Captained England in 8 Tests in India and Pakistan 1972–73 and played once *v* New Zealand 1973. Made over 20,000 runs, with 30 centuries; highest score 223 Glamorgan *v* Kent, Gravesend, 1966. Full back at rugby. Played violin for National Youth Orchestra of Wales. Cricket and rugby correspondent to *Sunday Tele-graph;* regular feature-writer for *The Cricketer*.
GALLERY SUBJECT: Bishan Bedi.

ROBIN Geoffrey MARLAR b. January 2, 1931, East-bourne, Sussex. Educated Harrow and Cambridge (cap-tain 1953). Captained Sussex 1955–59. Took almost 1000 wickets in first-class cricket with off-breaks. Best bowling 9 for 46 Sussex *v* Lancashire, Hove, 1955. Formerly lib-rarian to Duke of Norfolk. *Daily Telegraph* staff cricket and rugby writer before becoming cricket correspondent to *Sunday Times*. BBC sports broadcaster.
GALLERY SUBJECTS: Mike Brearley, Derek Under-wood.

MICHAEL Austin MELFORD b. November 9, 1916, St John's Wood, London. Educated Charterhouse and Oxford (half-Blue for athletics). War service with Royal Artillery on several fronts. Joined *Daily Telegraph* 1950, writing on cricket and rugby. *Sunday Telegraph's* senior cricket and rugby correspondent upon founding of that newspaper in 1961; has covered almost every major tour since. Became *Daily Telegraph's* chief cricket correspondent in 1975 upon the retirement of E. W. Swanton (to whom he was associate editor of *The World of Cricket* in 1966). Edited *Pick of The Cricketer* (1967) and *Fresh Pick of The Cricketer* (1969).
GALLERY SUBJECTS: Graeme Pollock, Barry Richards, Glenn Turner.

Henry Anthony (TONY) PAWSON b. August 22, 1921, Chertsey, Surrey. Educated Winchester and Oxford (captain 1948). War service with Rifle Brigade in North Africa, Italy and Austria. Debut Kent 1946 (making 90 *v* Hampshire). Stylish batsman, superb fieldsman. Highest score 150 Oxford University *v* Worcestershire, 1947. His 237 for Public Schools *v* Tufnell's XI before the war is a record at Lord's for a batsman under 16. Amateur football for Charlton Athletic; 10 amateur international caps. Formerly schoolmaster at Winchester. Cricket and football correspondent to *The Observer*. Deputy editor of *The Cricketer* 1971–72; still regular contributor. Books include *100 Years of the FA Cup* and *The Football Managers*.
GALLERY SUBJECT: Mike Denness.

Kumbla NIRANJAN PRABHU b. December 29, 1923, Kasargod, Kerala State, India. Educated Loyala College, and Presidency College, Madras. Played cricket, badminton, and tennis at college. Chief sports editor of *The Times of India* after having worked for *The New Chronicle,* Delhi and *The Melbourne Herald*. Covered Indian tours of England, Australia and West Indies, and 1959–60 Australian tour of Pakistan. India correspondent to *The Cricketer*.
GALLERY SUBJECTS: B. S. Chandrasekhar, G. R. Viswanath.

Raymond John (RAY) ROBINSON b. July 8, 1905, Brighton, Victoria, Australia. Long one of Australia's outstanding cricket-writers. Entered journalism in 1920s on *Melbourne Herald*. Two seasons as player in Melbourne sub-district cricket (with Nagel brothers). Australian correspondent to *The Cricketer* for 30 years. Has also written for newspapers in England and India. Nephew of Alec Robinson, captain of Goldfields XI *v* MCC 1924–25, and cousin of Dr George Robinson, captain of Western Australia *v* MCC 1946–47. Books include *Between Wickets* (1946), *From the Boundary* (1951), *Green Sprigs* (1954), *The Wildest Tests* (1972), *On Top Down Under* (1975).
GALLERY SUBJECTS: Ian Chappell, Rodney Marsh, Jeff Thomson.

ALAN ROSS b. May 6, 1922, Calcutta, India. Educated Haileybury and Oxford (contemporary of Kingsley Amis and Philip Larkin). War service took him on Arctic convoy route and to Germany. Cricket and squash for Oxford and Royal Navy. Author, poet, editor (of *London Magazine* since 1961), publisher. Cricket correspondent to *The Observer* for 21 years. Books include *Australia '55* (1955), *Cape Summer* (1957), *Through the Caribbean* (1960), *The Cricketer's Companion* (edited 1960), *Australia '63* (1963), *The West Indies at Lord's* (1963).
GALLERY SUBJECTS: Colin Cowdrey, John Snow.

GORDON John ROSS b. November 20, 1919, Blackheath, Kent. Educated Fairfield House and Colfe's. Commission in RAF during War. Wrote on cricket and rugby for the *Times* group 1947–66. Editor of *Playfair Cricket Annual* since 1954, and of *Playfair Cricket Monthly* from its inception in 1961 until its incorporation into *The Cricketer* in May 1973. Then became Executive Editor of *The Cricketer*. Books include *The Surrey Story* (1957), *The Testing Years* (1958), *Surrey: A History of County Cricket* (1971), *A History of Cricket* (1972). Sports consultant to Gillette Industries.
GALLERY SUBJECTS: Dennis Amiss, Keith Fletcher, Fred Titmus.

Michael John Knight (MIKE) SMITH b. June 30, 1933, Broughton Astley, Leicestershire. Educated Stamford School and Oxford (captain 1956). Record three centuries in Varsity matches. Debut Leicestershire 1951; with Warwickshire 1956. Captain Warwickshire 1957–67. 50 Tests; captain in 25: 2278 runs at 31.64, three centuries. Led England in Australia 1965–66, South Africa 1964–65, India 1963–64. Made 3245 runs in 1959 season. Almost 40,000 runs in a career ended by retirement autumn 1975; 69 centuries. Highest score 204 Commonwealth XI *v* Natal, 1960–61. Around 600 catches, mostly at short leg; record 52 for Warwickshire 1961. One England rugby cap.
GALLERY SUBJECT: Lance Gibbs.

Michael Hamilton (MIKE) STEVENSON b. June 13, 1927, Chinley, Cheshire. Educated Rydal and Cambridge (Blues 1949–52). Debut Derbyshire 1945. Right-hand batsman, left-arm slow bowler. Highest score 122 MCC *v* Cambridge University, Lord's, 1959. Best bowling 5 for 36 Free Foresters *v* Cambridge University, 1950. Former schoolmaster at Pocklington. Cricket-writer for *Daily Telegraph* and feature-writer for *The Cricketer*. Wrote *Yorkshire: A History of County Cricket* (1972).
GALLERY SUBJECTS: Geoffrey Boycott, Basil D'Oliveira, Farokh Engineer, Clive Lloyd, Majid Khan, M. J. K. Smith.

CLIVE TAYLOR b. April 5, 1927, West Norwood, London. Educated Clapham College. Employed by London suburban newspapers, *Morning Advertiser,* and Hayter's Sports Services before becoming freelance cricket-writer. *Sun* cricket correspondent since 1964. First tour 1958–59, covering MCC in Australia and New Zealand. Has accompanied most major tours since. Worked behind the scenes on several cricket books, the most outstanding being *D'Oliveira: An Autobiography* (1968). A useful batsman in club cricket.
GALLERY SUBJECT: John Jameson.